Biz Stone became an Internet entrepreneur in 1999. He went on to work for Google, helped to create both blogging and podcasting, and then co-invented Twitter. Before he was a tech star, Biz wrote books and articles about the social aspects of technology in the nascent days of the web. He regularly addresses large audiences as a visiting scholar at colleges or keynote speaker for companies and conferences. Most recently, Biz is founder and CEO of his newest venture, Jelly. He lives near San Francisco, California, with his wife and son.

Acclaim for *Things A Little Bird Told Me*:

'Biz gives away all his secrets to success. I advised him against it. If you're not inspired and informed by this book, then you haven't read it'   STEPHEN COLBERT

'Biz Stone's anything-but-ordinary journey both surprises and inspires. *Things A Little Bird Told Me* is a peek into a unique mind that, I'm happy to add, entertains us as well'

RON HOWARD

'Most tales of start-up success revolve around a lone genius out-manoeuvring the competition. But the story Biz Stone tells is a riveting – and often hilarious – break from that tradition: a story of collaboration, sharing, and the power of networks'

STEVEN JOHNSON, *New York Times*
bestselling author of *Where Good Ideas Come From*

'As someone who has personally experienced Biz's generosity and genius, I'm thrilled that readers of *Things A Little Bird Told Me* can now draw inspiration from his values and vision. A must-read for anyone who wants to tap their creative potential'

CHARLES BEST,
founder and CEO of DonorsChoose.org

THiNGS A LiTTLE BiRD TOLD ME

Confessions of the Creative Mind

BiZ STONE

MACMILLAN

First published 2014 by Grand Central Publishing

First published in the UK 2014 by Macmillan
an imprint of Pan Macmillan, a division of Macmillan Publishers Limited
Pan Macmillan, 20 New Wharf Road, London N1 9RR
Basingstoke and Oxford
Associated companies throughout the world
www.panmacmillan.com

ISBN 978-1-4472-7111-6 HB
ISBN 978-1-4472-7112-3 TPB

Visit www.panmacmillan.com to read more about all our books
and to buy them. You will also find features, author interviews and
news of any author events, and you can sign up for e-newsletters
so that you're always first to hear about our new releases.

For Livia

CONTENTS

CONTENTS

A GENIUS ENTITY

On October 7, 2003, a "Boston-based blogging entity" called Genius Labs announced it had been acquired by Google. The press release was picked up by various news outlets, and soon Genius Labs was added to Wikipedia's "List of Mergers and Acquisitions by Google." Once something makes it into Wikipedia, it is often repeated as fact. And in a way, it was fact. Genius Labs was an entity. It was me. The tale of how I got acquired—that is, hired—by Google says a lot about how I've made my way in the world.

INTRODUCTION

A year earlier, the future wasn't looking bright for the entity of me. My first startup, a site called Xanga that began with me and a group of my friends having the not-quite-refined idea that we wanted to "make a web company," wasn't what I'd hoped it would be. Tired of being broke in New York City— of all the cities to be broke in, it's really one of the worst—I quit. My girlfriend, Livia, and I retreated to my hometown of Wellesley, Massachusetts, with tens of thousands of dollars of credit card debt in tow. We moved into the basement of my mom's house. I had no job. I tried to sell an old copy of Photoshop on eBay (which is probably illegal), but no one bought it. At one point, I even asked for my job back at the startup—and my former colleagues said no.

The only bright spot in my so-called professional life was blogging. At the startup, we had used a piece of software from a company called Pyra, and I took an interest in the work of Pyra's co-founder, a guy named Evan Williams. I started writing my own blog and following Evan's, and in 1999, I was among the first to test-drive a new product Pyra had released: a web-logging tool called Blogger. To me, like lots of people, blogging was a revelation, even a revolution—a democratization of information on a whole new scale.

Xanga was a blogging community, but having left it, I was peripheral to that revolution, broke and directionless in my mom's basement. But my blog was another story. My blog was my alter ego. Full of total, almost hallucinogenic confidence, my blog was a fictional creation. It all began with the title, inspired by an old *Bugs Bunny* cartoon guest-starring Wile E. Coyote. In one scene, the ultrarefined coyote says, "Permit me to introduce myself," then presents a business card to Bugs with a flourish. It reads WILE E. COYOTE, GENIUS. By announcing himself as a genius on his business card, Wile E. Coyote epitomizes the spirit of the Silicon Valley entrepreneur. When you're starting a company, you sometimes have nothing more than an idea. And sometimes you don't even have the idea—just the supreme confidence that one day you will have an idea. You have to begin somewhere, so you declare yourself an entrepreneur just like Wile E. declares himself a genius. Then you make a business card and give yourself the title FOUNDER AND CEO.

I didn't have a company...yet. But in the spirit of Wile E., I christened my blog *Biz Stone, Genius.* I made up business cards that said the same. And in my posts, I made sure to play the part. Genius Biz claimed to be building inventions with infinite resources and a world-class team of scientists at his headquarters—naturally titled Genius Labs.

One of my posts in July 2002 read, "The scale-model of a Japanese superjet that is supposed to be able to fly twice as fast as the Concorde crashed during the test flight...I may have to sign various paperworks that will flow millions into further development of hybrid air transit."

Real-Life Biz was not investing in hybrid air transit. I did, however, manage to land a job as a "web specialist" at Wellesley College; Livia found a job, too. We rented a place near campus so I could walk to work. It wasn't so much an apartment as the attic of a house, but at least it wasn't my mother's basement.

My alter ego, Genius Biz, meanwhile, continued to exude

confidence, gaining more and more of a following. He was Buddy Love to my Professor Kelp. But as I sustained this charade, something started to happen. My posts weren't just wacky anymore. Some of the thoughts weren't in the character of a mad scientist; they were my own. As I continued to write about the web and think about how it might evolve, I started hitting on ideas that I would one day incorporate into my work. In September of 2003 I posted:

> My RSS reader [a syndicated news feed] is set to 255 characters. Maybe 255 is a new blog standard?...Seems limiting but if people are going to read many blogs a day on iPods and cell phones, maybe it's a good standard.

Little did I know how ideas like this, which seemed incidental at the time, would one day change the world. And I say this with all the humble understatement of a self-described genius.

Google acquired Evan Williams's company, Blogger, in early 2003. In the four years it had taken for blogging to evolve from a pastime of a few geeks into a household word, Ev and I had never met or even talked on the phone. But in the interim, I had interviewed him for an online magazine called *Web Review*, and I still had his email address. Now I worked up the confidence to contact him. I sent him an email congratulating him on the acquisition and saying, "I've always thought of myself as the missing seventh member of your team. If you ever think of hiring more people, let me know."

It turned out that, unbeknownst to me, Ev had been following my blog, too. In the tech world, that made us practically blood brothers. Though he was surrounded by some of the best engineers in the world, he needed someone who really understood social media—someone who saw that it was about people, not just technology—and he thought I was the guy.

He wrote back right away, saying, "Do you want to work here?"

I said, "Sure," and I thought it was a done deal. I had a new job on the West Coast. Easy peasy.

I didn't know it at the time, but behind the scenes Evan had to pull strings in order to hire me. Actually, they were more like ropes. Or cables—the kind that hold up suspension bridges. Google had a reputation for hiring only people with computer science degrees, preferably PhDs; they certainly didn't court college dropouts like me. Finally, the powers that be at Google begrudgingly agreed that Wayne Rosing, then Google's senior VP of engineering, would talk to me on the phone.

The day of the call, I sat in my attic apartment staring at the angular white Radio Shack phone I'd had since I was a kid. It had a cord. It was practically a collector's item. I'd never interviewed for a job before, and nobody had prepped me for this. Although I naively assumed that I already had the job, I at least understood that talking to Wayne Rosing was a big deal for someone in my position. I was nervous that I'd mess it up, and with good cause. A few days earlier, a woman from the human resources department had called me, and I'd joked around with her. When she asked me if I had a college degree, I told her I didn't but that I'd seen an ad on TV for where to get one. She didn't laugh. Clearly my instincts in this department weren't reliable. Real-Life Biz was consumed by self-doubt.

The phone rang, and as I reached for it, something came over me. In that instant I decided to abandon all the failure and hopelessness I'd been carrying around. Instead, I would fully embody my alter ego: the guy who ran Genius Labs. Genius Biz was on the job.

Wayne began by asking me about my experience. I guess he'd talked to the HR woman, because his first question was why I hadn't finished college. With utter confidence, I explained that I'd been offered a job as a book jacket designer, with the opportunity to work directly with an art director. I considered it an apprenticeship. As the interview went on, I acknowledged that my startup had been a failure—for me, at least—but explained that I'd left because the culture didn't fit my personality. In Silicon Valley, the experience of having crashed and burned at a startup had value. I told him about a book I'd written on blogging.

Then, in the middle of his questions, I said, "Hey, Wayne, where do you live?" That took him aback. I guess it sounded a little creepy.

"Why do you want to know where I live?" he asked.

"If I decide to take this job, I'll need to pick a good location," I said.

Decide to take this job. I didn't even know I was being audacious. But somehow it worked. I had the job. I was going to join Google. Evan invited me out to California to meet the team. With its seemingly limitless resources, scientists, and secret projects, Google was the place on earth most resembling my imagined Genius Labs.

A couple of years later, Ev and I would quit Google to start a company together. I had joined Google before the IPO, so I would be leaving lots of valuable shares behind. But my move to Silicon Valley wasn't about a cozy job—it was about taking a risk, imagining a future, and reinventing myself. My first startup had failed. But my next startup was Twitter.

This book is more than a rags-to-riches tale. It's a story about making something out of nothing, about merging your abilities with your ambitions, and about what you learn when you look at the world through a lens of infinite possibility. Plain hard work is good and important, but it is ideas that drive us, as individuals, companies, nations, and a global community. Creativity is what makes us unique, inspired, and fulfilled. This book is about how to tap into and harness the creativity in and around us all.

I'm not a genius, but I've always had faith in myself and, more important, in humanity. The greatest skill I possessed and developed over the years was the ability to listen to people: the nerds of Google, the disgruntled users of Twitter, my respected colleagues, and, always, my lovely wife. What that taught me, in the course of helping to found and lead Twitter for over five years, and during my time at startups before then, was that the technology that appears to change our lives is, at its core, not a miracle of invention or engineering. No matter how many machines we added to the network or how sophisticated the algorithms got, what I worked on and witnessed at Twitter was and continues to be a triumph not of technology but of humanity. I saw that there are good people everywhere. I realized that a company can build a business, do good in society, and have fun. These three goals can run alongside one another, without being dominated by the bottom line. People, given the right tools, can accomplish amazing things. We can change our lives. We can change the world.

The personal stories in this book—which come from my childhood, my career, and my life—are about opportunity, creativity, failure, empathy, altruism, vulnerability, ambition, ignorance, knowledge, relationships, respect, what I've learned along the way, and how I've come to see humanity. The insights gained from these experiences have given me a unique perspective on business and how to define success in the twenty-first century, on happiness and the human condition. That may sound pretty ambitious, but when we're taking a break from developing hybrid air transit, we aim high here at Genius Labs. I don't pretend to know all the answers. Actually, strike that: I just might pretend to know all the answers. What better way to get a closer look at the questions?

1

HOW HARD CAN IT BE?

So, in a single phone call, Genius Biz had landed a job at Google pre-IPO. Or so he thought.

After my conversation with Wayne Rosing, I thought I would just drive to California and start my new life. In anticipation of that, my would-be employers had asked me to fly out to the Google offices in Mountain View to meet them in person and finalize the details.

At this point Evan Williams was my champion. Having

never laid eyes on me, he had pushed Google to hire me, and now he was meeting me at the airport to take me to my new workplace. I had no idea what a big part of my life Evan would become, and that one day he and I would start Twitter together. At that point I was just grateful for the ride.

I arrived at the San Francisco airport on an early flight, and when Evan picked me up in his yellow Subaru, Jason Goldman, his right-hand man at Blogger, was in the passenger seat. I jumped in the backseat, and as we drove to Google, I was immediately jokey about my plane ride. As is my wont, I probably made some inappropriate remarks, because I remember Evan and Jason laughing and saying, "We just met this guy five seconds ago and *this* is where he's going with his banter?" I tend to come on a little strong, but I could see that they were pleasant and casual and had a nice rapport. I wasn't surprised. I'd been reading Evan's blog for so many years that I knew there was a thoughtful person in there. He was wearing jeans, a T-shirt, and sunglasses. He had a slight build, a big smile, and he drove like a maniac. Goldman has a memorable laugh. He usually hits a high note at the end.

Because Google hadn't gone public yet, it was still a startup, but it was already several years in and considered very successful. There was no Googleplex yet, just a bunch of people working in leased stucco buildings.

Evan showed me the place and introduced me to the Blogger team. After making the rounds at the office, he and I went to a party in Mountain View for a bit; then we drove up to San Francisco to have dinner at an Italian restaurant in the Marina District with his mother, who was in town, and his girlfriend.

After dinner and plenty of wine, I was ready to go to my hotel—I had more meetings at Google the next day and I was still on East Coast time—but Evan had other plans for us.

"Let's go to the Mission! I'll show you some of my favorite bars."

Evan, his girlfriend, and I kept the party going at a bar called Doc's Clock. I ordered a whiskey neat, and the bartender poured me a full juice glass.

"Wow," I said, marveling at the quantity.

"They have a good pour here," Ev said.

By last call, at 1:40, we'd all had plenty to drink. Ev, who was blitzed, leaned back in his chair, opened his arms wide, and said, "Biz, all this could be yours." We had a table in the rear, and I was sitting with my back to the wall. From my vantage point, I could see the whole bar, a dimly lit, hipster-friendly dive bar, not much more.

"Really?" I said sarcastically. "This?"

Evan put his head down on the table. We were done.

The next day, I had twelve meetings with various Google executives. It became immediately clear to me that these "meetings" were in fact interviews. Turned out this job I thought I already had wasn't yet mine. I was smack in the middle of Google's famously rigorous application process.

But I swear what got me through was the certainty that the job was mine. Channeling my Genius Labs persona wasn't the only strategy I had up my sleeve.

Before I got on the phone with Wayne Rosing, I'd never

applied for a real job before. I had no idea how an interview, phone or live, was supposed to go. But as I've said, I did have one thing going for me: the well-established confidence and chutzpah of Biz Stone, Genius.

Still, you can print that on a business card or type it on a website, but you can't just summon that attitude out of thin air. So there was something I did before the phone interview that helped me summon Genius Biz. Here's how it worked: In the days leading up to that phone call, I took the idea of working on the Blogger team at Google and let it bounce around in my head. Back then I liked to take a slow jog from my apartment, which was practically on the Wellesley campus, down to Lake Waban and around the two-plus-mile dirt path. As I ran, I pictured myself in a strange office somewhere near San Francisco, with a bunch of guys I'd never met, doing the work I wanted to do.

Most of Google was entirely made up of computer science PhDs. They were very talented at building software. The role I envisioned for myself was to humanize Blogger. I would take over its home page—the company's official blog—and make the Help area into a product called "Blogger Knowledge," where I would highlight features of the service. I would give a voice and brand to Blogger. (Though I didn't know it at the time, this is what I would find myself doing at every company I joined: embodying and communicating the spirit of the thing we were creating.)

This is a useful exercise with any problem or idea. Visualize what you want to see happen for yourself in the next two years. What is it? *I want to have my own design studio. I want to join a startup. I want to make a cat video that goes viral on YouTube.* (Can't hurt to aim high.) As you're working out or going for a walk, let that concept bump around in there. Don't come up with anything specific. The goal isn't to solve anything. If you take an idea and just hold it in your head, you unconsciously start to do things that advance you toward that goal. It kinda works. It did for me.

———

Now I was at those offices I had imagined. They were a little different from my fantasy; I'd expected…I don't know, a Googleplex maybe, and instead there was a bunch of non-descript buildings; Blogger was in building number π—but I'd already been working for Blogger in my head for at least a week. Besides, it was hard to be intimidated when nobody seemed to understand what job they were interviewing me for. It all made sense to me and Evan, but the human resources department at Google was a little baffled by my job description. My explanation that I was going to add humanity to the product only seemed to confuse them further. In interviews, the Google staff was known to make engineers solve difficult coding problems on a whiteboard. They had no idea what to ask me. My hobbies? Adding to the general fuzziness of the interviews, Evan and I had been out 'til 3:00 or 4:00 a.m.

In the first meeting, when a woman said, "Thanks for coming in. Can I get you anything?" I said, "Yes. Do you have an aspirin?" I'm pretty sure on the list of job interviewee "don'ts," immediately exposing your hangover ranks high.

One of the guys who interviewed me asked, "Do you know

why Google acquired Blogger?" He was genuinely curious. At that point Google had acquired Deja.com's Usenet discussions, but this was its first real acquisition of a company with employees. My answer was simple, if not necessarily correct. I said, "Well, it's the other half of Search. Google searches web pages. Blogger makes web pages. It gives you more to search."

By the fifth interview, I asked a guy, "Do you know why you're interviewing me?" He said, "No. I only started here two days ago." I'm pretty sure on the list of job interviewer "don'ts," that's also pretty high up there. Maybe that meant we were well matched.

Regardless, when all was said and done, the job that had never been mine finally was.

With no small help from Evan, I'd manufactured this opportunity without a college education, much less a higher degree; without working my way up a ladder; and with a failure or two under my belt for good measure. I wasn't a shoo-in; I wasn't anything. But I did have experience in one particular area: creating my own opportunities.

——

I discovered early on that it was better to make my own destiny. As a kid, I spent a bunch of time playing in the yard alone, but one of my favorite things was to go down into our basement and "invent things." My grandfather built telephones for American Telephone and Telegraph in Boston from 1925 to 1965. He passed before I was born, but my mother never cleared out her father's work stuff. In our basement were his workbench, all his tools, and a giant

apothecary-type arrangement of various s̱
wires, and the like—everything my grandfatı.
build and repair rotary telephones. I'd go dow
pretend to be inventing wondrous contraptions in ı
underground laboratory.

My mom's best friend, Kathy, had a husband, Bob, who was an electrician. His basement, as far as I was concerned, was another laboratory. The real deal. Whenever we visited their home, I would walk straight in and say, "Bob, let's go invent some stuff in the lab. I have a few ideas." I distinctly remember having a revelatory thought that with two empty soda bottles and some hoses, I could rig a contraption that would allow me to breathe underwater.

When I told Bob the idea, he said, "You mean SCUBA?"

I told him the name needed more thought and insisted we get to work. He diplomatically said we'd need an air compressor and some other things he didn't have and suggested we build a battery-powered light mounted on an upside-down coffee can instead. It wouldn't allow me to breathe underwater, but if it had batteries and wires, I was all for it. Another time, I wanted to invent a flying contraption. Instead, we hooked a speaker up to a battery. We slipped flat copper strips into a plastic mat and connected them to the speaker so that when you stepped on the mat, it activated the speaker and made a horrible buzzing noise. I brought it home and slipped it under the area rug next to my bed. That night I crawled into bed and yelled, "Mom, you forgot to kiss me good night!"

"Aw, so sweet!" she said. She came into the room, stepped on the rug, activated the alarm, and nearly had a heart attack.

7

"My invention worked!" I crowed.

Perhaps to channel this energy, my mom enrolled me in a program called Boy Rangers. Not the Boy Scouts. Not the Cub Scouts. Some obscure other program called Boy Rangers. It was like the Betamax of scouting programs. Not only did I not want to be in the Boy Rangers, but every week I had to bring "wampum" to the program—*I had to pay*. Also, my parents had divorced when I was a toddler, and my dad lived a few towns over, but he might as well have lived in Istanbul. My parents were oil and water, so we barely ever saw my father. As it happened, the Boy Rangers was a father-son thing. Every week, all the other boys had their dads with them, and I attended solo. If there was a merit badge for "rubbing it in," they all would have earned it without trying.

Anyway, the Boy Rangers was modeled after Native American tribes. In order to advance from Paleface through Papoose, Brave, Warrior, and eventually to Hi-Pa-Nac (which sounds like an anti-cholesterol drug but is actually some sort of chieftain) we had to create our own feathered headdresses, learn how to tie knots, and memorize various tribal slogans. You know, cool-kid stuff. I was stuck in Boy Rangers from age six to ten, all those critical years when most boys were playing Little League baseball, Pee Wee football, and all the other sports. I wasn't very driven to master the Boy Rangers skills, but the leaders always gave everyone the patches anyway. The other kids had their patches sewn onto their khaki shirts, but my mom attached mine with safety pins.

As a struggling single mom, the most important thing my mom did for me, my sister Mandy, and my two half-sisters,

Sofia and Samantha, was to keep us in Wellesley, where she'd grown up. The town had become very affluent, and the public school system was one of the best in the country. My mom had gone through the Wellesley school system and loved it. She was determined that we have similarly good experiences.

To me, all my friends were rich. It seemed that they assumed I came from a wealthy family, too, but at various times, we were on welfare. I remember the gigantic slabs of government-issued cheese. I was on a school lunch program for low-income families, which was good because it meant I didn't need lunch money, but it was bad because of the way it worked. To buy lunch, most students bought lunch tickets. Those tickets were green. To get my lunch tickets, I had to go to a special office once a week to be issued five gray lunch tickets. When other kids asked why my lunch tickets were gray, I made jokes about their green tickets. I suppose I started developing a sense of humor and a certain attitude to deal with the obvious differences in our lifestyles. I would even raid the Lost and Found box so I could find a Ralph Lauren Polo shirt—something other than the same jeans and T-shirt that I pretty much exclusively wore otherwise. Most of my socks and underwear were marked "Irregular." My mom did her best, and she managed to keep us in Wellesley, in a school system that happened to be receptive to my particular brand of creativity.

When I got to high school, all my friends were nerds. But I knew from TV and the movies that a good way to expand my social crowd would be to play on a sports team. I was naturally athletic, and from all my years in the Boy Rangers, I was really good at tying half-hitches and sheepshanks, but I'd never tried a team sport. The basketball court had all these crazy lines on the ground. All the other kids seemed to know where you were allowed to stand and for how long. I just stood there. Then, in the football tryouts, there were all these rules. How did it work? How many chances did we get? And how was I supposed to know when I was on the wrong side of the field? I was confused and nervous, which made me even more confused. Before I went to the baseball tryouts, I wised up and did a little research. But there was no way to make up for all the lost time. In this situation, the visualization technique I used to land the job at Blogger wouldn't have worked. Even if I'd been aware of the strategy at the time, I would have visualized myself making a thousand home runs and then stood by and watched while all the other kids scored them. Unsurprisingly, I didn't make any of the sports teams. That's when I decided to take matters into my own hands.

A little investigating told me that there was one sport my high school did not offer at the time: lacrosse. If none of the other kids had any experience playing lacrosse, then everyone would feel as confused as I did. It would be a level playing field. So I asked the school administration whether, if I found a coach and enough boys, we could start a lacrosse team. The answer was yes. So that's what I did. After all that apparent ineptitude, I emerged as a decent lacrosse player, I was elected captain, and we were a pretty good team (though I still preferred the company of the nerds to the athletes).

The determination that led me to create a new sports team taught me an important lesson: opportunity is manufactured.

My dictionary defines *opportunity* as a set of circumstances that makes it possible to do something. The world has conditioned us to wait for opportunity, have the good sense to spot it, and hope to strike at the appropriate time. But if opportunity is just a set of circumstances, why are we waiting around for the stars to align? Rather than waiting and pouncing with a high degree of failure, you might as well go ahead and create the set of circumstances on your own. If you make the opportunity, you'll be first in position to take advantage of it.

It wasn't until later that I realized that this is the core of entrepreneurship—being the person who makes something happen for yourself. But it's also true for all forms of success, in all parts of life. People say success is a combination of work and luck, and in that equation, luck is the piece that is out of your hands. But as you create opportunities for yourself, your odds at the lottery go way up.

In high school I'd learned how fulfilling it was to make my own opportunities, and I assumed I'd be able to do the same in college. I graduated high school in 1992 and cobbled together a bunch of local scholarships to cover my first year of college at Northeastern University. Knowing the funding would run out, I landed a scholarship for excellence in the arts, which gave me a free ride at the University of Massachusetts, Boston.

But college didn't turn out to be all I'd envisioned. Every day, I commuted an hour from my mother's house to the UMass campus, a maze of concrete that was rumored to have been designed by builders who specialized in prisons. One of the first things I wanted to do there was produce *The White Rose*, a play based on an early anti-Nazi movement in Germany. But the woman who ran the theater department told me my only option was to attend her class and be a part of whatever play she had picked. Hmm. That wasn't what I had in mind.

On the side, I got a job moving heavy boxes in an old mansion on Beacon Hill for the publisher Little, Brown and Company. I carried boxes of books from the attic of the mansion down to the lobby. It was the mid-nineties, and the publisher's art department was transitioning from spray glue to Photoshop. They even had an old Photostat machine in its own little darkroom—a huge and expensive machine that did the same job as a ninety-nine-dollar scanner. I knew my way around a Mac, and designing book jackets looked like fun. So one day, when the entire art department went out to lunch, I snooped around until I found a transmittal sheet for a book that listed the title, subtitle, author, and a brief summary of what the editorial department wanted for the jacket. The book was *Midnight Riders: The Story of the Allman Brothers Band*, by Scott Freeman. I sat down at one of the workstations and created a book cover for it. On a dark background, I put "Midnight Riders" in tall, green type. Then I found a picture of the band, also very dark, that looked good below the title. When I was done, I printed it out, matted it, and slipped it in with the other cover designs headed to the sales and editorial departments in the New York office for approval. Then I went back to moving boxes.

Two days later, when the art director came back from presenting designs in New York, he asked, "Who designed this cover?" I told him I had. He said, "You? The box kid?" I explained that I knew computers, and that I was attending college on a scholarship for the arts. He offered me a full-time job as a designer on the spot. The New York office had picked my jacket to use on the book. Looking back, it wasn't very good, but they chose it.

I was being offered an honest-to-goodness full-time job. Should I take it? College so far had been a disappointment. (My experience there reminds me of a Dutch phrase that an entrepreneur I visited in Amsterdam once told me: "He who stands up gets his head chopped off.") And here I was being handed an opportunity to work directly with the art director, who would turn out to be a master. The way I saw it, people went to college in order to be qualified to get a job like the one I was being offered. Basically, I was skipping three grades. Besides, I'd learn more here, doing what I wanted to do, than drifting anonymously through college. So I dropped out of college to work at Little, Brown, one of the best decisions of my life.

I'm not advocating dropping out. I could have entered college with more focus in the first place, or I could have tried to change my experience when I got there. But taking a job that I'd won through my initiative was another way of controlling my destiny. This, as I see it, was an example of manufacturing my own opportunities.

This is why starting a lacrosse team, producing a play, launching your own company, or actively building the company you work for is all more creatively fulfilling and potentially lucrative than simply doing what is expected of you. Believing in yourself, the genius you, means you have confidence in your ideas *before they even exist.* In order to have a vision for a business, or for your own potential, you must allocate space for that vision. *I want to play on a sports team. I didn't make it on a team. How can I reconcile these truths? I don't like my job, but I love this one tiny piece of it, so how can I do that instead?* Real opportunities in the world aren't listed on job boards, and they don't pop up in your in-box with the subject line: Great Opportunity Could Be Yours. Inventing your dream is the first and biggest step toward making it come true. Once you realize this simple truth, a whole new world of possibilities opens up in front of you.

That modus operandi is what brought me to Google in 2003.

I'd landed at Google, but Real-Life Biz was still working out the kinks. Genius Labs was a nonentity, Livia and I still had tens of thousands of dollars in credit card debt, my car wasn't up for the cross-country drive, and I was on my way to an opportunity I'd manufactured out of nothing but a unique blend of confidence and desperation.

I wanted a bigger car, a Toyota Matrix, for the move across the country, so I went to a dealership to trade in our old Corolla. I said to the dealer, "I have this Corolla, but I don't have any money. Can I give you the car and get a payment plan for the rest?"

He said, "For five thousand dollars down—"

I interrupted him. "I really don't have any money. I have no money. Nothing. Zippo."

He said, "For two thousand dollars down—"

I politely interrupted again, "If I had some money, I'd give it to you, but I don't. I've no money, no access to money, and my credit cards are completely maxed out."

So he took my Corolla and gave me a financing deal that even he admitted was terrible. Time for another visualization.

I thought, *Here's to my future self, who will pay for all of this.*

2

EVERY DAY'S A NEW DAY

Renewables are just what they sound like: naturally replenished resources. They're inexhaustible. In spite of the earth's depleting reserves, don't you feel better already, thinking about renewables? The idea of replenishment is such a relief. *There's more where that came from. We won't run out. This life that we're trying to live is sustainable.* This is an important concept when we think about the world's resources, but it's also applicable to our work and lives, and it came into play in my eventual decision to leave Google.

I worked on Blogger at Google for two years, and up until the initial public offering, Livia and I were still deeply in debt. Our living situation was less than ideal. In fact, it was less than mediocre. Before we moved to San Francisco we had asked Evan and Jason where we should live. The most obvious choice was downtown Mountain View, near where the Google offices were located. But Jason and Evan were self-proclaimed San Francisco snobs, so they told us, "You gotta live in the Mission, man. That's where it's at."

We could tell that the Mission was too gritty for us. It was in that phase between down-and-out and up-and-coming, where the hipsters had moved in but there were still gunshots at night—possibly directed toward the hipsters. For people like Ev, who grew up in Nebraska fantasizing about the big city, it was cool being the city mouse. But Livy had grown up in New York City in the seventies. She'd had enough of living in the city; she wanted to be the country mouse. To move to yet another city and pick a transitional district with lingering gang territories would have rubbed salt in the wound. Then we read about a really nice neighborhood that was Mission adjacent: Potrero Hill. From the pictures we found online, it seemed to have a cute street with an old-school deli, a family-owned grocery store, a corner bookstore, and probably a savings-and-loan run by George Bailey, from the looks of it.

Still searching online, I found a fifteen-hundred-square-foot loft in Potrero Hill for thirteen hundred dollars a month. Holy crap! I'd always wanted to live in a loft. And the apartment was number 1A. We'd be on the ground floor—no more walking up to the attic. We'd walk out our front door and be right in charming Potrero Hill.

Fingers crossed, I called the landlord. It was still available! I agreed to rent it on the spot. We felt so pleased with ourselves to be driving west with our affordable, cool loft waiting for us.

What we failed to take into account was the "hill" part of Potrero Hill. Downtown Potrero Hill is at the base of the north slope. Our new apartment, we discovered on arrival, was on the south slope. The only way to get from one side to the other was to walk up and over a hill steeper than a ski slope. I'm all for cardio, but I wasn't about to climb that hill every time I wanted an overpriced scone, which I couldn't afford anyway.

As for the cool loft building we'd anticipated, it was squeezed between two housing projects, overlooking the highway and a rendering plant, where I'm pretty sure they were making glue out of seagulls, or something along those lines. Our picture windows looked out onto an industrial wasteland.

Also, it was a live/work loft, and the guy next door was in a band. Guess what instrument he played? Did you guess drums? Good for you! He played loud, crazy music all night, and kept a barking pitbull as his companion.

But the real kicker was the mistake we'd made in assuming our apartment, 1A, would be on the ground floor. The building was built into the side of a cliff, so the numbers were basically reversed—you entered on the ninth floor and the floors went down from there. We had rented a ninth-floor walk-down. Each day began with us clambering up nine double-height flights of metal stairs.

Every morning, I commuted to my new job in Mountain View, a pretty town with shops and cafés and a weekly farmers' market. It would have been perfect for us. Our rent there would have been even lower, and I could have biked to work. Anyhoo, that's not what we did.

Livia and I didn't have any furniture for a year and a half. Our credit card debt was a black hole that ate all our income. And when Google gave out one thousand dollars in cash to every employee at Christmastime, I stopped on the way home that day to recklessly spend most of the bonus on a TV. We put the TV on the floor and used its box for a dining table. Otherwise, we were living hand to mouth. We'd brought only our cats and whatever else would fit in our Toyota Matrix. There hadn't been room in the car or money left over for luxuries—like, say, a bed. We slept upstairs on the bedroom floor. At least it was carpeted.

At Google, when word got around that I was sleeping on the floor, some colleagues passed around a coffee can and raised eight hundred dollars for me to buy a bed. It was an amazingly kind gesture, and I was touched and grateful. However, I had no choice but to misallocate the funds and put them all toward my obscene car payments, which were several months overdue. As for the rest of our furniture, I brought home two garish, multicolor Google beanbag chairs. We sat in those beanbags and slept on the carpet for over a year—until I finally got some dough from Google.

I joined Blogger in September 2003. On August 19, 2004, Google finally had its much-anticipated public offering. The options I was granted as part of my hiring package were on a four-year vesting schedule. I had the right to buy them for a dime per share. By the time Google went public, I was one year vested, and the value per share quickly rose to over one hundred dollars. By the next year, it had nearly tripled. Every month, I was allowed to exercise more of my stock options, so I would pick up the phone, ask a guy on the other end to "sell, please," put down the phone, and say, "Livia, I just made ten thousand dollars." Little by little, we chipped away at our credit card debt.

But something was missing. Something I'd learned to love in my first job, the one I dropped out of college for, working for the art director at Little, Brown.

On my first official day of work as a designer at Little, Brown, I walked into the art director's office, and he silently beckoned me over to his desk. Without speaking or turning around, he reached his left hand over his right shoulder and plucked a book from the shelf. Like a Jedi Master, he never took his eyes off me. The book he had selected was a Pantone color swatch book, and it must have been the one he wanted, because he started looking through it. I stood quietly and watched as he slowly flipped through pages and pages of colors. Finally, he stopped in the range of the light browns and tans. He found what he wanted and tore out one of the little perforated swatches. He put it down on his desk, placed one finger on it, and wordlessly slid the chocolate-colored swatch slowly toward me. He then stated drily, "That's how I take my coffee."

Oh my God. I dropped out of college for this. I gave up an awesome free-ride scholarship. And now I have to go to Dunkin' Donuts and ask the lady if she can do the coffee...

In three seconds, all those thoughts went through my head. As I was considering how to replicate that color at the local café with just the right amount of cream, the art director burst into laughter.

"I'm kidding! What kind of asshole do you think I am?" And so began my apprenticeship in graphic design and my introduction to a new way of thinking. The director, Steve Snider, and I worked side by side for over two years.

Book cover design teaches you that for any one project, there are infinite approaches. There were several factors at play in jacket design. A jacket had to satisfy us, the designers, artistically. It also had to please the author and the editorial department by doing justice to the content. It had to appeal to Sales and Marketing in terms of grabbing attention, and positioning and promoting the book. Sometimes designers were frustrated when their work was turned down by one department or the other. "Idiots. Fools," they'd mutter, storming around the office. "This is a brilliant design." And maybe it was. But our colleagues in Sales and Editorial had experience in their jobs, and I learned from Steve to assume that their concerns were legitimate.

Steve told me that once, for a biography of Ralph Lauren, he'd had a brilliant idea. He wanted to put out six different jackets, each in a solid, preppy color with the Polo logo in the upper left in a contrasting color. That would be it. Ralph Lauren's photo might be on the back. It would have been so iconic. But Editorial nixed it. So that was that. Steve was still proud of the idea, but he understood that his opinion wasn't the be-all and end-all.

For a book called *The Total Package*, by Thomas Hine, which deconstructed the world of product packaging, I took a little cardboard box of powdered pudding. I opened it up, ungluing the seams, and flattened it out. I made a jacket that mimicked the deconstructed box, with its registration lines and that little rainbow where they test the ink colors. I was really proud of the final product. But, instead, they used an elegant black-and-white jacket with product shapes on it. My jacket wasn't used, but the work wasn't wasted. I put it in my portfolio. I still thought it was cool.

Steve taught me that having a cover turned down wasn't a problem. It was an opportunity. My job wasn't only to be an artist, creating work that pleased me. The challenge was to come up with a design that I loved *and* that Sales and Editorial thought was perfect. That was the true goal. "Your goals should be bigger than your ego," Steve used to tell me. When I satisfied every department, only then would I have really succeeded in nailing a cover.

When Steve and I were stuck, we'd try to inspire ourselves. We'd take a precut matte frame and hold it up against different things around the office. Would the wood grain of a credenza make a good background? How about the blue sky outside? (Steve Snider would later use a blue sky with white clouds as the background for David Foster Wallace's *Infinite Jest*.)

Sometimes there were restrictions that limited our options. We'd be told, "For this book, you have to use this photo. It was taken by the editor's sister. It's nonnegotiable." And the art would suck.

I'd say, "Great, gimme that one." Then I'd turn the art sideways and blow it up eight hundred percent. Now it was cool. There was always another way to go. My creativity wasn't limited to five designs per book, or any other number. There was always another potential cover. I quickly learned not to care about the hard work that had been wasted. I didn't take rejection personally. My creativity was limitless. I wanted to come up with another idea. *I got a million of these*, I thought. *I could do this all day long!* It was a matter of attitude.

Graphic design is an excellent preparation for any profession because it teaches you that for any one problem, there are infinite potential solutions. Too often we hesitate to stray from our first idea, or from what we already know. But the solution isn't necessarily what is in front of us, or what has worked in the past. For example, if we cling to fossil fuels as the best and only energy source, we're doomed. My introduction to design challenged me to take a new approach today, and every day after.

Creativity is a renewable resource. Challenge yourself every day. Be as creative as you like, as often as you want, because you can never run out. Experience and curiosity drive us to make unexpected, offbeat connections. It is these nonlinear steps that often lead to the greatest work.

Steve became my mentor. He drove me in to work every morning, and we became friends, playing tennis together on weekends. He was more than thirty years older than me, but we were a good match: I didn't have a dad growing up; he had two daughters, and he'd always wanted a son. Eventually he started bringing me with him to present covers to the New York office. On the way, I'd ask him a million questions, not just about design, but about life. *How did you know when to propose to your wife? How much money did you ask for at your first job?* Asking questions is free. Do it!

With Steve's encouragement and confidence in me, I left Little, Brown to start a freelance business doing book design. It was the late nineties, so it was inevitable that I would soon expand my services to include website design. Every new business then included website design. I could have started a dry-cleaning service, and the sign would have read ALTERATIONS/WEBSITE DESIGN. When my friends graduated college and decided to form a web company, I was already designing and building websites. We started Xanga together. Learning design with Steve set me on the path that led me where I am today.

The notion that creativity is infinite drove my everyday energy, but that idea rose to the fore in 2005, when I was still at Google, working on Blogger, having finally climbed out of the debt that had plagued me for my entire adult life.

I was endlessly inspired by the characters at Google. There was Simon Quellen Field, a self-named older guy whom I'd met my very first day at orientation. I asked him what he was going to be doing at Google and he said, "I don't know. Something that requires a PhD." Simon had a big gray beard, a long gray ponytail, and a live parrot perched on his shoulder. He claimed that he owned a mountain in Los Altos, lived on top of it, and had a huge aviary and parrot farm.

During lunch, a guy named Woldemar (a.k.a. "He Who Is Sometimes Mistaken for He Who Shall Not Be Named") would juggle by himself. I'd go over and talk to him: "Don't you feel weird juggling here?"

"Nope."

"I'd feel nervous and embarrassed."

"Well, I don't."

"Okay, see you later, Woldemar."

Misha was squat, with a potbelly, a beard, and a thick Russian accent. He tracked me down when I posted a paper on the Google intranet. (The paper considered that, like it or hate it, when you go for a job interview or on a date, people are going to Google you. You might as well take ownership of that. I suggested that Google let people convert the search results on their names into a social networking profile page, editing the results, and expanding from there. I called it Google Persona. I still think it's a pretty good idea, but it's up on the shelf, next to Steve's Ralph Lauren book jackets.) Anyway, Misha read my post and took an interest in me. He hunted me down and said, "Biz, come. We take walk."

Should I take a walk with this Russian guy? Why not?

So from then on, Misha and I would take strolls. We'd amble by the parrot guy and the juggling guy, and he would say things like "Biz, I invent new way to present time." It was guys like Misha who made Google work.

Despite the welcome financial stability of the job and the endlessly fascinating characters, there was something missing from my work at Blogger: I didn't have a chance to challenge myself every day.

One of the ways I tried to fulfill that urge was to regularly brainstorm with Evan about what we might do next if we were to leave Google. One afternoon in 2005, he and I were carpooling home to San Francisco from Google in Mountain View. Ev was driving his yellow Subaru wagon, and I was riding shotgun.

"You know how people can record their voice in the web browser with Flash if they have a built-in microphone?" I asked.

"Yes," Ev said.

"Well, we could build something that lets people record whatever they want. Then we could convert that to an MP3 on our servers."

"Sure."

"Okay," I said. "I think I have a genius idea."

"I'll be the judge of that." Evan will listen to any idea I have, but he's not one to get overexcited. He's thoughtful, analytical.

We were driving through the northbound dot-com traffic on Highway 101, around San Mateo. I took a deep breath and went on.

"It seems like iPods are getting super popular. We could make it really easy for regular people to create recordings—talking, singing, interviews, or whatever the hell they want—

by talking to a web page. Say lots of people do this, and we convert all their random recordings to files, MP3s."

"Go on," Evan said.

"We collect all these recordings in one place and make them available. Then other people can subscribe to whomever they like." I explained to him how it might work technically, and how the recordings would sync between their computers and their iPods.

At last Ev's eyes opened wide and his jaw dropped. His "holy shit, that's a good idea" face.

"So you see what I'm saying. We could basically make a service that democratizes audio in the same way Blogger democratizes the making of web pages. Anyone can have what is essentially his or her own radio show. Other people can easily get that show onto their iPods, so they can listen to all this stuff whenever they want. It could be a whole thing."

You know I'm excited when I say, "It could be a *whole thing.*"

"You might be on to something." Evan is a tough nut to crack, but I'd cracked him.

"I told you I had a genius idea."

———

Once we got back to the city and started researching this notion, we found out I wasn't quite as genius as I thought—other people had already thought of this and were calling it podcasting. Still, we thought there was a wide-open market for a mainstream, consumer, web-branded podcasting service.

Evan consulted with his friend Noah Glass, who had been

working in this space—recording voices in the browser using Flash. Noah had named his service Audioblogger, because it posted people's recordings to a blog. But he hadn't yet put together anything that made it easy to subscribe to these recordings and get them on an iPod.

One night, Ev called while Livia and I were cooking dinner at our "loft" in Potrero Hill.

He said, "Noah and I are hashing out the idea you had in the car. Come join us."

I glanced over at the broccoli, potatoes, and fake meat stew simmering on the stove. I was hungry. It looked good. "Nah," I said. "You guys go ahead without me." It's moments like this that make and break fortunes in Silicon Valley. Stupid broccoli.

Because Google had acquired Blogger, Evan had already made his fortune and was free to do whatever he wanted. (Yes, he bought a silver Porsche after the Google IPO. You can't blame a kid from Nebraska for buying a toy like that when he becomes a multimillionaire.) The next thing he did was to quit Google, team up with Noah, and launch a podcasting company called Odeo.

A short time after that first call Ev told me that he had raised five million dollars to build Odeo with Noah. It had all happened so quickly, and suddenly I felt like I'd missed the boat. They'd started the company without me. Sure, Google was a great place to be. It was a hot company. I had no boss. I was earning maximum bonuses. I didn't have to go in to work if I didn't want to. I had two years of options left to vest. I could relax at Google and make millions of dollars. Or I could quit in order to work on a startup that might not succeed. (Spoiler: it failed.) But I wanted to be challenged every day.

Think about your work situation. Do you treat your creativity like a fossil fuel—a limited resource that must be conserved—or have you harnessed the unending power of the sun? Are you in an environment where creativity thrives? Is there room for new ideas every day? Can you make room?

I had moved out to California to work with Evan Williams, not with Google. That was more important to me than options or job security. I couldn't sit around waiting for my options to vest when I had a chance to be a part of a startup with Evan. Sure, I was bringing a human side to Blogger, but the website was already well on its way. Leaving a stable, comfortable job is like starting again from scratch. It's not easy, and it may not work the first time, but it can ultimately lead to greater things. I needed a new source of energy. It was time to hack on a new thing.

I called Evan and said, "I want to quit here and work at Odeo."

He said, "Awesome."

So I quit Google.

Starting over is one of the hardest leaps to make in life. Security, stability, safety—it's scary, if not downright irresponsible, to leave these behind. I was at Google in 2003 and I might still be there now. But I had faith in my future self. (After all, my once-future self had finally managed to pay off the Toyota Matrix.) I could help build something new.

By this point, after we had paid off our debt at last, Livia and I had broken the lease on our ninth-floor walk-down in Potrero Hill, rented a condo in Palo Alto, and I'd started biking to work. After two years of commuting from San Francisco to Mountain View, now I was driving from Palo Alto back up to the city to the Odeo offices. I'd reversed my commute.

And so we moved again. This time I asked Livia to decide where we should live, since my track record on this was so poor. She chose Berkeley, and because we were tired of landlords who wouldn't allow us to bring along our menagerie of rescue animals, we wanted to own our home. Livy was the director of WildCare in San Rafael, a wild animal ER. What happens there is very different from a vet's office, where people might bring in an obese housecat and try to help it live to be seventy. When people find injured animals—squirrels, hawks, owls, skunks—they bring them to WildCare for help. But unlike with dogs and cats, there's no established protocol for some of the cases. (How do you make a prosthetic leg for a seagull?) And WildCare's a nonprofit, so often it's improvising with whatever's been donated. A tiny mouse with a broken leg? They fix it with dental equipment from the seventies. Livy was saving lives. She's wired to help others, and her life of altruism absolutely inspires me.

At the time, we ourselves were caring for two rescue dogs, two rescue cats, and a rescue tortoise. At various times we also had foster bunnies, crows, and rodents of varying sizes and shapes. So we took all the money we'd saved and used it as a down payment. We bought a little eight-hundred-square-foot house that had been built as the maid's quarters to a bigger house. Half that square footage was the garage.

I'll never forget celebrating my thirty-second birthday in that house. Livy, who did most of the work taking care of our animals, had gone to a medical conference for almost a week, and I was left to manage the animals by myself. It gave me a taste of the work she did professionally and often in our home. One of the dogs was prone to seizures. The other was anxious and attacked people. There was a cat that had been hit by a car and didn't know when it was dripping poop. Livy left me with all of them plus, in the garage, five baby bunnies whose mother had been killed. They were really cute, but they were still nursing and had to be fed milk through a syringe. Then there were the crows, wintering in a giant aviary I'd crammed into the gap between our Berkeley house and the neighbor's fence. The cage was big enough for them, but I had to stoop when I went in to feed them a stinky combination of dead smelt and fruit. Livy had said, "Whatever you do, don't rile up the crows. They have broken wings. They shouldn't flap them." So I had to be quiet and gentle while I unclipped the food tray, replaced it with a new one, and reclipped it. But the stupid thing would not unclip. Wasps, attracted to the food, swarmed around me. I had to stay calm—I couldn't rile the crows—during a twenty-minute wasp fest while I replaced the tray.

The second day Livy was gone was my birthday. At two o'clock that morning, Pedro, the older dog, started having a seizure. I ran upstairs in nothing but my tighty whiteys and found him with his tongue hanging out, eyes bulging. I thought he was dying. I picked him up and held him the way I thought I'd seen Livy do. He exploded dog diarrhea all over me. Then the phone rang. It was Livy, returning my desperate call for help. Holding the dog, covered in shit, I tried to answer without getting shit on the phone. Just then, the seizure stopped. "We're fine," I told Livy and quickly hung up. As I cleaned myself up, Pedro ran around like a puppy, overjoyed to be alive.

With the new house and a startup salary at Odeo, Livy and I were instantly back on our way to credit card debt. But hey, it wouldn't have been a true leap of faith in myself if the stakes hadn't been high. I had opted for risk and creativity, and that choice would serve me...eventually.

3

THE KINGS OF PODCASTING ABDICATE

I never regretted leaving Google, but our new company was ultimately doomed. The reason why was an important lesson for me that went beyond the basic tenets of business and entrepreneurship.

Eventually we had a dozen or more people working on Odeo. Podcasting was becoming a popular activity, at least with early adopter geeky types. Whenever something became popular on the web, there was a risk that Apple or another megacompany would swoop in with powerful development teams and dominate the market. But it never occurred to us that Apple would be interested in podcasting. Why would they want to incorporate such a fringe interest into their main operating system? At the time, Apple seemed uninterested in social software.

To our surprise, in late 2005, Apple introduced podcasting right inside iTunes. Where we saw it as a way for people to exchange information, Apple saw it as a way for people to listen to professional, radio-type entertainment on demand. That was an application that made sense for them. And as it turned out, they were right about how podcasting would most commonly be used.

This development could have been a fatal blow to our startup. Why would anyone go to Odeo when they could just use iTunes? But this lesson—to watch out for the big guys—wasn't one I needed to learn, and it isn't my point. Ev had a smart idea to refocus Odeo on one specific feature of podcasting—as a way for people to get recommendations based on what they or people with similar tastes liked. We felt strongly that Apple wouldn't bother with the social aspect of podcasting. They didn't have photo communities around their photo app. We could save our skins by working on something iTunes probably wouldn't do.

It was the right business move. However, by that point it didn't matter, because there was something else that condemned Odeo, something more devastating than a corporate competitor with deep pockets.

Neither Ev nor I, nor (I suspect) several other members of our team, were actually interested in podcasts. We ourselves didn't listen to them. We didn't record our own. The truth is that good audio requires good production. Listening to Terry Gross is great, but listening to some dude in his basement drone on about XML for an hour with a low-quality mike and no sound production is pretty arduous.

We lacked something that is the key to a successful startup, and it was bigger than sound quality. It was emotional investment. If you don't love what you're building, if you're not an avid user yourself, then you will most likely fail even if you're doing everything else right.

I can't work on anything I'm not interested in. One time, in high school, when I had to write a paper for a political science class, I got stymied. The topics were boring, and I couldn't bring myself to write the paper. I was going to fail, or get a bad grade, unless I could find a way to enjoy the task.

Then I decided that I would write about vigilantism, using *Batman* comic books as my primary source materials. As soon as I came up with this topic, which was completely interesting to me, I wrote the paper in one sitting.

Evan and I hadn't yet figured out that we didn't care enough about podcasting. When Apple launched podcasting, Evan wrote a memo and circulated it to some of the team. It was a very well-written plan for making Odeo a success by focusing on what we called social discovery—those recommendations that a service generates based on previously liked material, the way Amazon does with books. When I read Evan's memo, I knew it was a good plan and would probably work. One night that same week, Ev and I went for sushi and whiskey at a place in San Francisco we both liked. I brought up his memo. I had something I wanted to ask him.

"Ev, I really liked what you wrote. It's really smart and it will work."

"Thanks."

"If we execute the vision you laid out, we will become the kings of podcasting." I gave a great flourish when I said "kings of podcasting." I made it sound very kingly.

"Wow, you think it was that good?" Ev looked pleased with himself.

"Yes," I said, "but I have a question for you."

"What?"

"Do you *want* to be the king of podcasting?" I asked, because this was the question I'd been asking myself.

Ev took a sip of his whiskey, set the drink down, and then laughed. "No, I totally don't want to be the king of podcasting," he said.

"Neither do I," I told him. I knew the weight of what we were saying. How could we do this if it wasn't something we were enthusiastic about? But at the same time I was excited at this revelation. *If we weren't engaged, we couldn't go on.*

Realizing the same thing I had, Ev wasn't laughing for long. He put his head in his hands and let out a groan of frustration. I could tell it meant "You're right. Now what?"

Evan is probably one of the few people in the world who can work with me. As I've mentioned, he gives me the freedom to be crazy and have crazy ideas. If I were to say, "Just for a minute, assume there's no gravity," Evan would say, "Go on." He values my brainstorming capabilities and intuition and understands that for all the extraneous blather, there might be a legit idea in there. That's why we're a good team. I'm in the clouds, and he's grounded.

Ev has always been patient when I want to think out loud—so that evening, I did.

"We could just throw Odeo out and start on some completely different idea. We have a good team and a bunch of money still in the bank."

Ev perked up at that idea at first, but then he scowled. "As much as I'd love to do that, we raised this money from investors for the purpose of building a podcasting company. We can't use other people's money to dabble with various other projects that may or may not work."

He had a good point. I wouldn't have felt comfortable doing that, either. So I continued to toss out suggestions.

"Maybe we should just bail completely, then. Just admit to ourselves, the team, the investors, the board—everybody—that we don't want to do it anymore. Then we could sell the company to somebody who actually likes podcasting."

Ev decided to think about it more seriously. We finished up our dinner and called it a day.

After a week or so, Ev resolved to tell the board of directors that he didn't intend to continue being the CEO of Odeo. If they wanted, he would help them find somebody to take his place. But the board didn't want that. The investors had put their money on Evan as much as on the promise of the idea. It was decided that the best thing to do would be to hire a broker to find a buyer for Odeo.

It was during this period that Evan made a decision that would forever alter the trajectory of my life. He announced to the team that the board was engaged in shopping for a buyer for Odeo. Then he suggested a "hackathon." Mostly as a morale booster, Ev suggested that a skeleton crew continue to support Odeo, so it worked for the people who were currently using it, while the rest of us "hacked": we would team up in pairs and have two weeks to build anything we wanted. This was a great idea because it encouraged all of us to pursue the ideas that most compelled us. If Evan devised this challenge as a response to our shared apathy for podcasting, and because he suspected that passion would spark our best work, I completely agreed. And we were both right.

There was a programmer at Odeo named Jack Dorsey, and the two of us had hit it off from the start. Jack was a quiet type, but it was easy to make him laugh. We hung out on the weekends, talking about other ideas we'd had for startups or things we'd built that had failed, and we collaborated on mini projects within Odeo. It was like in school when you're asked to pick a partner and you know you're going to pick your best friend. I knew off the bat that I wanted to pair up with Jack for the hackathon. But what were we going to work on?

The story gets a little muddled here, because right after Ev announced the hackathon, it was lunchtime. A bunch of people went out together. I wasn't there, but apparently Jack had an audience of people and described to them what he wanted to work on. When he came back to the office, he asked if I wanted to partner up.

I said, "Yeah, I was assuming we would. What do you want to do? Maybe picture-blogging? It has to be something constrained." We didn't have much time so I wanted to keep the project simple and elegant. "We could do the Phonternet, a little internet that you would look at just on phones. Like a MySpace for phones."

Jack said, "Those are cool. I have an idea." He brought me over to his desktop to explain. Together we looked at his buddy list on AOL Instant Messenger (AIM). There was a little feature called Status. It was there so you could say that you were away from your desk or out to lunch, and so on, so people would know why you weren't responding to their messages.

About half a dozen of Jack's friends had set their status. Jack pointed out that instead of just saying "Away" or "Busy" or something like that, people were playing with the status message. One of them had changed it to "Feeling blah," and another had made it "Listening to the White Stripes." Or something like that. Jack said that he liked having a sense of how his friends were feeling or what they were up to just by glancing at these status messages. He asked me if I thought we should build something similar—a way to post a status message and a way to see your friends' status messages.

I loved the simplicity and constraint of the idea. In fact, it reminded me of two short-format blogging projects I had previously launched but failed to grow into anything worthwhile. Before I went to Google, I'd come up with something called Sideblogger, which would allow you to post quick, smaller musings alongside your more thoughtful blog posts. And while I was at Google, I'd worked on Blogger on the Go, short-format blogging from a mobile phone.

As a kid, Jack had a fascination with the way cities worked and the way taxis were dispatched. If you could tune into that, you could tune into the pulse of the city. He liked the way all these status updates would map society in a similar way—how software could capture and reflect human behavior. I was the social side of the equation. I was interested in what enabled special interactions between people.

Then Jack said, "It's still Odeo, because you can attach a snippet of audio to go along with the text entry."

I said, "No, if we're going to do this, let's do it super simple, and be done with audio."

Jack laughed. "Okay, no audio."

I said, "I'll start mocking stuff up."

He said, "I'll figure out how to build it simply."

At first we thought we were building a way to update your status to friends by phone. The website would just be a Welcome screen where people registered their phone numbers. But who would come to a random website and willingly give us their phone number? We threw that out, and I started brainstorming different ways we could allow people to update their status—a web interface, an instant message. But we were talking about a status report on what people were up to when they were "away" from their regular lives. Because of this, the most likely application was a text message from a mobile phone.

If someone sent a status report to us from their phone, we wouldn't have to ask for their phone number—we'd already have it. Sign-up, at first, would be by text only. Then we figured out that we should let people update their status on the web, and the update would still go to people's phones.

So that was our project. Jack and I decided that we would build a way to exchange simple status updates by SMS (text message). I would design the web interface, a place where people could see the messages they were exchanging, and Jack would figure out how to hook texting up to the web, and vice versa. It was simple, and I was far more excited about it than I'd ever been about podcasting.

———

Noah Glass, co-founder of Odeo with Ev, had named the podcasting service. The name Odeo is cool for that service because it sounds like "audio," and it's visually appealing. So Jack and I asked Noah for help coming up with a name for our project.

At the time, we were working in funky offices at 164 South Park. It was near the opening of the park, just across from a Shell gas station. The space had been built in a courtyard formed by the exteriors of some other buildings, so the interior walls had once been outside; one of them still had the original window in it, allowing us to peek into the neighboring building. The front had wood floors and a high ceiling, so it was big and open. Some people thought it was cool, but I wouldn't have picked it. The carpeting was worn out, a stained pale green; the basement had mice; and the back opened onto an alley hosting homeless people, syringes, and human poop. If you go over there now, it's pretty fancy. There are condos, restaurants, and venture capital firms, but it was gritty at the time.

Whoever was there before us had some kind of shop in the back, with a plywood floor and storage for recycling bins. You could close the sliding glass doors of that back room and talk without bothering the engineers. This lair was where Noah was often to be found.

"We want a name that feels quick and urgent," one of us said during a meeting in that back room. The name had to capture the idea that your phone would buzz in your pocket with simple updates from friends *right now*. Noah had come up with a short list of twitchy words.

"How about Jitter?" Noah said.

"It's a little overcaffeinated, don't you think?" I said.

"Or Flitter, or Twitter, or Skitter," Noah was on his computer now, looking up words that rhymed with Jitter.

"Twitter," I repeated enthusiastically. It made me think of the light sound of birds chirping. It also meant short or trivial conversation. "You guys, it's so perfect."

Noah was partial to Jitter or Jitterbug. He thought we should be targeting kids. I didn't want to target kids. We didn't know anything about kids. I didn't even like those two words together: *target* and *kids*.

This was just a hack project, and I was so wed to the name Twitter, that the guys either agreed or caved easily. In retrospect, it was a shockingly short and incidental conversation.

———

During the two-week hackathon, Jack and I taught ourselves the rules of using a short code, the five-digit phone number people would use to send us their texts. We wanted the short code to spell Twttr. Jack found the registration page and typed it in to see if it was available, but it was already owned by *Teen People* magazine. We tried out different variations (twitr, etc.), but then we decided to just forget that. We'd pick one that was easy to remember, and to input with one hand. We settled on 40404. It was the perfect distance for your thumb to travel on the phones of the time. For a hot second we contemplated naming the service 40404. Jack loved the aesthetic simplicity, but Twitter was much better. We decided to stick with Twitter.

While Jack worked on the back end, I build a mock-up that showed how the service would function. As Jack and I worked, we rolled up to each other's desks in roll-y chairs to talk, or I'd spin my screen around to face him, saying, "How does this design look?" I kept it stark and simple, mostly white. We both liked that. Usually I was excited, and Jack was calm. I made jokes; he laughed. I knelt on top of my chair and spun around like a kid while I talked nonstop, repeating myself if I was excited. Jack listened quietly. Or I lay on the ground talking while Jack sat properly in his chair, his hands clasped or flat on the table, nearly expressionless except when he chuckled. Sometimes we went for walk-and-talks, walking around the city and talking through ideas.

I talk a lot. "No, that's a bad idea. Wait, it's a good idea. Is it a good idea?" It was the same with Ev and Jack. I'd brainstorm, and they'd filter. They were both patient enough to listen to the junk—or I didn't give them a chance to get a word in edgewise.

At the end of our two weeks, Jack and still I didn't have a working prototype, but I had mocked up a fake web version of Twitter. At the hackathon presentation, our colleagues had come up with some of their own projects. One of them (done by Adam Rugel, I think) made fun of what everyone knew Jack and I were building. It was called Friendstalker, and if I remember correctly, it consolidated your friends' postings into one place so you could aggregate all your friends' online activity. Florian Weber did something called Off Da Chains. I have no memory of what it was supposed to be. Another team came up with a concept for group communication.

When it was our turn to present Twitter to Odeo employees, I stood up and demo'd the "service" using a laptop hooked up to a projector. It didn't matter that the programming wasn't done yet. The demo let me click through the experience of sending a status message by phone and seeing it posted on the web.

The first screen showed a webpage. At the top it read, "What are you doing?" and had a place where you could enter your status. I typed, "giving a demo." Then I clicked on Submit, and another screen came up showing my status at the top:

giving a demo

Below it were mock posts from everyone else using the service. Then there was a line, and below that were messages from my favorite people.

Then I said, "Here's Jack's phone." I clicked to the next slide, which showed a picture of his phone with my text message, "giving a demo," Photoshopped onto it.

Then I showed his phone sending "eating lunch" to 40404. The next slide was another web screen, where we could now see that Jack was eating lunch.

That was it. Our demo showed how the communication would work between phones and the web. I titled it "Twitter, an Odeo thingy."

The team was less than impressed by what we had built. Someone said it was too simple and needed something more interesting, like video or pictures. We said that the whole point was that it was supposed to be really simple. On the whole, the project wasn't very well received.

Nonetheless, Jack and I couldn't stop thinking about it. The whole time I was on the subway going into work, all I would think about was ideas for Twitter, features for the user interface, questions I wanted to run by Jack. *Oh my God, if we did that, then we could do this. Wait, that won't work. What if we did this?* The train couldn't go fast enough. I would hurry from

Montgomery Station to South Park to get to work as soon as possible. Every day, more momentum built. It was an idea I couldn't shake. That was the feeling. Later on, I would put a finger on this as emotional engagement, but I didn't define it at the time. I was too busy living it.

Jack and I loved working together, and we were excited to keep going until we had a functioning version of the idea that we could try out. After our presentation, in a private conversation with Evan, Jack and I asked if we could continue together on Twitter. Evan gave us permission. We would get a real prototype up and running in a few weeks. That two-week hackathon project was the birth of Twitter.

Our offices consisted of an open loft with an upper deck in the back of the space. Ev and I had desks up there, near each other. I often walked over to his desk to bother him. It was the only way to pull information out of his quiet Nebraskan head.

A week or so after the hackathon, I walked over, sat down on an inflatable yoga ball, and asked him what was up. He told me that the board had been unsuccessful in its search for a buyer for Odeo. Apparently we weren't the only people who lacked enthusiasm for podcasting. If nobody bought the company, it would mean real failure—the money we had spent would be lost, and the investors would probably never again want to invest in anything we did. This was why I always made a point of checking in with Evan. Important information, ideas, and worries festered within. He never proactively shared.

"I've thought of every avenue there is," he said. "There's no way out."

We sat there in silence for a few moments—with him unmoving, me bouncing slightly up and down. Then I looked at him. I didn't know how much money he had, but I figured he was rich from selling Blogger to Google for stock before Google's public offering.

I said, "There is a buyer for Odeo if we want one."

"Have you been listening to me?" Ev asked. "I just told you, there is no buyer."

"Yeah there is: you," I said. "What if *you* bought Odeo? Then the investors would get their money back, our reputations would be intact, and we'd be free to do whatever we wanted."

Ev thought there was some merit to the idea; he might even have considered it himself before I mentioned it, but it was unconventional, to say the least. Entrepreneurs don't generally raise money from venture capitalists, create a faltering business, and then buy the business from the VCs. If buying his way out of failure were perceived negatively, it might hurt Ev's reputation and career.

Then I suggested that we announce publicly that Ev and I were starting a new company together as a startup incubator, and we planned to acquire Odeo. Since everything wonderful seems obvious in retrospect, we would call the company Obvious.

This was an easy plan for me to endorse, considering I didn't have any money to offer—though nobody outside my immediate circle of friends (except Visa) knew this. In fact, I had already borrowed money to pay off my credit cards, again. My interest rate was a whopping 22 percent, and when I did the math, I realized that if I paid the monthly minimum, it would take me more than two hundred years to pay off the debt. My grandchildren would be paying down my credit card bill. So I borrowed money from Ev. We set it up as a legitimate loan with interest, but he gave me a much more humane rate.

My financial limitations aside, adding my name to the deal seemed to make Evan feel more comfortable. This way, if everything went south I'd share the blame with him. We'd both look like chumps. (As it happened, things went north.)

Obvious offered to buy Odeo and all its various side projects (including Twitter, which nobody thought was worthwhile) from the investors. Of the five million dollars raised for Odeo, there were still three million left. Obvious offered to buy the company for two million, plus a little more, so the investors got all their money back and then some. It worked out well; the investors were satisfied. Eventually Ev found a buyer for the Odeo technology. A Canadian company bought it for one million dollars, which went back to Ev. If you do the math, that means Ev bought Twitter for a million dollars—a real bargain, considering what it's worth today.

I had moved from Little, Brown in Boston; to starting my own business as a web designer; to a brief stint at Xanga; to a job at Wellesley College; to Google; to Odeo; and now to Obvious, where I was already at work on a project that captivated me in a way that nothing ever had. By spring of 2006 this little project finally attracted the interest of the rest of the company. The newly minted employees of Obvious set to work on Twitter, and we made good progress.

The moment we got the texting part to interact with the web part of Twitter, I was working from home and IM'ing with Jack. It was March 21, 2006, at 11:47 a.m. When Jack's maiden Tweet—what we were then calling an update—appeared on my screen, I was so excited that I IM'd him Alexander Graham Bell's famous words to his assistant when he made the first phone call:

Mr. Watson, come here—I want you.

I later discovered that I didn't get the quote exactly right, but that thrill of discovery was the spirit we all felt in the early days of getting Twitter up and running. I had left Google for Odeo in search of fertile ground for creativity. What I hadn't found at Odeo was there from the start with Twitter. Of course, I had been dying to get the Blogger job at Google. And I had been eager to leave for Odeo. It felt like real passion. But what I felt now was different. That high—the excitement of invention; the effortless flow of ideas, good and bad; the conviction that what you are doing is meaningful and cool—it's a little like falling in love. I didn't know exactly what I was looking for until it was standing right in front of me.

At first we didn't buy the domain name twitter.com. A bird enthusiast already owned it. Instead we set up the service at twttr.com. At some point Noah suggested we spell it that way: Twttr. Like Flickr. But I wanted our name to be a genuine English dictionary word. Later, when we bought the domain name from the bird guy, my blog post was "We bought the vowels."

For a long time the home page stayed as we'd first designed

it, displaying the most recent Tweets from everyone using the service. Actually, that was the basis for much of the flack we got. *Who's Joey B, and why do I care what he's having for breakfast?* What we eventually learned is that *someone* does care what Joey B is having for breakfast. The Follow button let those people identify themselves.

When we first came up with the idea for "followers," there was an argument about the terminology. Some thought we should call it Listen. But it wasn't listening; it was reading updates. "Subscribe" was too boring. I argued for "Follow."

"You're following this person like you *follow* the news and you *follow* football games. You *follow* Biz Stone."

That thrill—the joy that I never found in podcasting—would continue throughout the birth of Twitter, but there is one particular day that stands out in my memory. It was early in the prototyping phase, before we had launched. Only a few of us were using the service. My wife and I were living in our tiny box of a house in Berkeley. There was a heat wave. I had chosen this day to do some home improvements.

Remembering the old episodes of *This Old House* that I liked to watch as a kid, I figured I'd rip out all the once-white wall-to-wall carpeting in our house to expose the attractive hardwood floors beneath. With scissors, I made a big gash in the carpet. Then I started the arduous process of ripping it up from the nails that held it down at the edges. It wasn't until I had already ruined the carpeting that I discovered there was no hardwood floor underneath.

Still, there was no turning back now; I decided to pull up the carpeting anyway. Hunched over, sweating from the heat wave, and cursing my stupidity, I felt my mobile phone buzz in the front pocket of my jeans. I fumbled to take it out and read a Tweet from Evan Williams:

Sipping pinot noir after a massage in Napa Valley.

My situation at precisely that moment, and its incongruence with Ev's, made me laugh out loud. My wife thought I had lost my mind. In truth, I was not just amused; I was enlightened. In that moment, I realized why my other startups had failed and why Twitter was going to work. Twitter brought me joy. I was laughing out loud on a Sunday afternoon using the application that I had spent many days and nights working on. I was passionate about this project.

That hot day in Berkeley stands out in my memory because it was the day I realized the value of emotional investment. You know in your heart something's worth pursuing; you're not sure exactly why, but it doesn't matter. Success isn't guaranteed, but failure is certain if you aren't truly emotionally invested in your work.

That commitment was a critical element that would carry us through the toughest challenges ahead. At first Twitter was ridiculed. Someone called it the *Seinfeld* of the internet: a website about nothing. That was intended as an insult. Undaunted, I added this remark to the rotation of testimonials on the site's home page. I took it as a compliment. *Seinfeld* is maybe the funniest show of all time! No matter how many times Twitter broke—and we repeatedly had to struggle to fix it and explain the cause of the crash yet again—my faith in the idea kept me going. I could bear any struggle if my work was bringing me joy. My passion for the project made me immune to all the things people thought were stupid and useless about Twitter. I, who had had no desire to be a king of podcasting, was very excited to be a creator of Twitter. This was a powerful lesson.

So often people follow a career path without thinking about what really inspires them. How many people graduate college, see that lawyers and doctors get paid a lot, and follow that route, only to discover that they hate it? I think about the comic Demetri Martin, who often appears on *The Daily Show*. He went to law school at NYU, but instead of being a lawyer, he ended up a quirky comedian who plays the ukulele and uses puppets in his act.

Adopting a career because it's lucrative, or because your parents want you to, or because it falls into your lap, can sometimes work out, but often, after you settle in, it starts to feel wrong. It's like someone else punched the GPS coordinates into your phone. You're locked onto your course, but you don't even know where you're going. When the route doesn't feel right, when your autopilot is leading you astray, then you must question your destination. *Hey! Who put "law degree" in my phone?* Zoom out, take a high-altitude view of what's going on in your life, and start thinking about where you really want to go. See the whole geography—the roads, the traffic, the destination. Do you like where you are? Do you like the end point? Is changing things a matter of replotting your final destination, or are you on the wrong map altogether?

A GPS is an awesome tool, but if you aren't the one inputting the data, you can't rely on it to guide you. The world is a big place, and you can't approach it as if it's been preprogrammed. Give yourself the chance to change the route in search of emotional engagement.

If you don't wake up excited for the day ahead, and you think you're on the wrong path, how do you find your way? I always tell people to back into it. Imagine working on something you love. Describe it to yourself. Don't focus on how much money you want. Instead, think about this: What type of people surround you? What sort of work are they doing? How do you get to work? What adjectives would people use to describe what you do?

Maybe your ideal situation is to be in a funky office space near the ocean. There are bikes hung on the wall right outside so you can go for a ride in the middle of the day. Maybe there are even office surfboards. People are laughing. Maybe, describing your fantasy, you say, "We have a lot of fun during the day, but sometimes we work really hard."

What job is like that? Maybe you should consider working at a small ad agency. The place sounds like a creative shop of some kind.

Once true passion hits you, you can recognize all the times in your life when you were chasing the wrong dream. And after you've experienced that sustained fulfillment, you'll never want to settle for anything less.

4

A SHORT LESSON IN CONSTRAINT

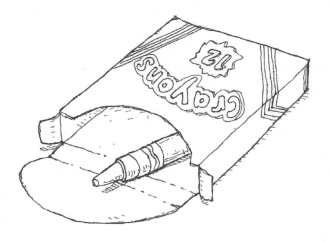

One of the first decisions we made about Twitter, something that never changed, was that each message would be limited to 140 characters or fewer.

Constraint inspires creativity. Blank spaces are difficult to fill, but the smallest prompt can send us in fantastic new directions.

There are stories supporting this all over the place. I read somewhere that when he was making the movie *Jaws*, Steven Spielberg wanted to build a giant, realistic mechanical shark in order to shoot scenes of the scary beast attacking people. But making that full-size shark became a budgeting nightmare, so Spielberg came up with a low-budget solution. He decided to shoot from the shark's point of view, underwater, looking hungrily up at the tasty legs of the oblivious swimmers. Guess what? *Way* scarier. Those shots came about because the director's budget was constrained. The *New York Times* recently joked about how today's *Jaws* would look, opening on Shia LaBeouf playing a rock star and a supermodel wife: "We zoom in for a super-close-up of the shark's enormous computer-generated teeth, in 3-D, chomping them both in half." Lame.

Another Spielberg story: When Harrison Ford was shooting *Raiders of the Lost Ark*, three months of filming in Tunisia gave the actor a terrible case of the runs. When it came time to shoot a long, drawn-out sword battle, Ford, desperate to call it a day, suggested that when faced with the sword-flashing enemy, he simply pull out his pistol and shoot the guy. This improvised solution became one of the movie's best, funniest, and most iconic scenes.

On special occasions when I was a child, my family went to a restaurant in Waltham, Massachusetts, called The Chateau. There were velvet paintings of Frank Sinatra on the walls, and the menus were paper placemats. To distract me while we waited for our food to arrive, my mom would flip over the placemat, take a pen from her checkbook, and tell me I could draw.

"What should I draw?" I'd say.

"Draw anything," my mother would answer.

But I would stare at the blank page and ask her again, "What should I draw?"

Finally she'd say, "Draw a dump truck." That did the trick. I'd start drawing right away. And it wasn't necessarily a dump truck. In fact, it probably wasn't ever a dump truck. But limiting my options gave me a place to start. I felt the same way when I started designing book covers. I liked being told it was a two-color jacket, or that we couldn't afford to buy art. Or that whatever the jacket looked like, it had to include a dump truck.

In business, constraints emerge from the time you have to finish a project, the money you have to invest in it, the people you have to build it, or the space to you have complete it. These limitations, counterintuitively, can actually enhance productivity and creativity. Think about the question "How was your day?" The answer is almost always "Fine." But putting constraints on the question—"How was your lunch with Steve?"—yields a much more interesting answer.

At a dinner once, I sat next to Hermann Hauser, the guy whose company created ARM, the technology that powers the chips that are in practically all cell phones. He's a billionaire from Silicon Fen, the high-tech business region around Cambridge, England. Hermann said to me, "I'll tell you how we came upon the perfect chip for mobile. It was an accident. You know what I gave my team? No money, no time, and no resources."

Given their limitations, the engineers came up with a low-power chip that wasn't very good for PCs. But it turned out to be perfect for cell phones. Now that chip dominates the market.

Embrace your constraints, whether they are creative, physical, economic, or self-imposed. They are provocative. They are challenging. They wake you up. They make you more creative. They make you better.

———

My favorite artist is the sculptor Andy Goldsworthy. He uses exclusively natural materials to make site-specific sculptures, usually out in the wild. Each piece is an impossibly difficult, arduous task, an exercise in endurance. He'll use his bare hands to break the inch-thick ice off the top of a lake, then will work nonstop to arrange the broken pieces into a sphere bigger than a man. Or he'll build a snaking stone wall through a forest in Scotland that starts with a tiny pebble and gets increasingly larger as it winds its way, ending with hulking boulders. Or he'll collect red leaves, tie their stems together, and thread them through the trees. His projects blow away in the wind, melt in the sun, or crumble into dust. Their ephemerality adds to their beauty.

What do Goldsworthy's self-imposed constraints say about how we can live our lives? He has so little to work with, and from that simplicity come great peace and beauty. Most lives are filled with too much stuff. What do you really need to make a life? What can you live without? People think of constraint as giving something up instead of gaining something. But if you give away your Xbox, you gain back all the hours it used to suck from your life. Embrace constraint. What you get in return is the art and craft of editing your own life, weeding out what is and isn't necessary.

It was the constraint of the two-week hackathon that led to the creation of Twitter. And from day one, the length of a Tweet was always limited, although it didn't start at 140 characters.

When we began, we knew that the international text messaging standard limit was 160 characters. This was true for all carriers everywhere—it had to do with bandwidth constraints, or something technical like that. The only reason people don't talk about the 160-character limit on texts these days is because now the carriers just stitch two texts together if they run over that limit.

We wanted Twitter to be device agnostic, so that on any crappy mobile phone you could see and write a Tweet, no problem. This meant using the 160-character limit that already existed for texts. At first we gave a user the entire 160 characters, but into that space we automatically inserted a space, a colon, and your username. You got whatever was left.

One day I raised an issue with Jack. "Wait a minute," I said. "It's not fair. Some people get more room to twitter than others, depending on the length of their names."

Jack said, "Good point. We should standardize our own

thing." We decided that fifteen characters was about the right amount of space for a username. Then, instead of giving people the remaining 145 characters, we gave them 140. We just picked a number. There was no numerological magic. The standard could just as easily have been 145. It was just simpler to make it 140. The next day, Jack sent out an email to let everyone know that we were standardizing at 140.

The 140-character limit was an accidental PR hook from the start. It was such a big mystery. Why 140? Was it the number at which people were the most creative? Reporters always joked, "I'm excited to interview you guys. I might have to go over a hundred forty characters." The novelty of it made for a good icebreaker, but our answers to the question were probably more interesting than the journalists expected. We talked about simplicity, constraint, universal access, and our desire to be device agnostic. It was a good thread to pull.

Beyond the practical reasons, I believe the limited length of a Tweet contributed to Twitter's success. From the start, the character length was one of the most hated and loved and talked-about features of Twitter. In the first six months, we saw the advent of Twitter haikus and something people called "twooshes," updates that used exactly 140 characters. The constraint was inspiring. It lent a consistent rhythm and poetry to the service. And if that weren't self-limiting enough, in 2006 we partnered with *Smith* magazine to help it launch its Six-Word Memoir Project on Twitter:

> *A character with character limits characters.*
>
> —Biz Stone

One hundred forty is not a magic number. But imposing a limit brought people together. It was a challenge. You are writing the story of your life. Edit it as you go. In 140 characters, what's worth saying? How could we express ourselves to each other in this space? How much could be said, and how much would be left unsaid? Twitter was not a place for diatribes or monologues, so what was the point? What's worth saying? What don't we need? That provocation made riddlers and poets of all of us.

5

HUMANS LEARN TO FLOCK

In March of 2007, I attended the South by Southwest Interactive (SXSWi) conference in Austin for the fifth time. Back then the event was primarily known for its movie and music divisions. Interactive, which was my beat, was just a bunch of nerds looking out of place next to the leather-jacketed musicians checking in at every hotel lobby reception desk. It would be a stretch to say that we were the cool kids.

Still, lots of San Francisco Bay Area geeks attended SXSW

to learn about new stuff and meet up with like-minded sorts. There were lectures and panels during the day, but more important was what happened at night. Some startup was always throwing a party. In a weird phenomenon where you had to travel fifteen hundred miles to get a drink with some-one whose office was down the block from yours, these parties were great places to meet up with industry colleagues whom you never saw in the Bay Area because you were constantly working.

That spring there were plenty of people saying that Twitter was stupid and useless. What was the point of software that helped you share the minutiae of your day? But by then there were also about forty-five thousand people signed up and using Twitter. Most of the folks who were active on the service were early adopters, those same Bay Area geeks who love to try out any new technology mostly because it's new.

Back at Blogger, we'd always hosted a party at SXSW. But Twitter wasn't established enough to warrant a party. When we were strategizing our presence, Evan tossed out the idea of creating visual displays in the hallways instead of in the conference room. This was a stroke of brilliance. Tradition-ally, companies set up booths on the floor of a giant confer-ence room, but we knew from past experience that most of the daytime action at the festival took place in the hallways between the lecture rooms. People congregated there to chat about talks they'd heard, products they'd seen, events their friends were attending, and where the party was that night. They sat down against the walls with their laptops to answer emails and catch up with work.

We decided we wanted to put up a bunch of big flatscreen monitors in the hallways. We would build a Tweet visualizer, where people attending the festival could watch their SXSW Tweets appear in real time.

Nobody had ever put displays up in the *hallways* of the conference before. We went back and forth with the festival organizers, negotiating the use of this space. We had never, ever paid a dime to market Twitter, and this was going to cost us ten thousand dollars—a lot of money for us at the time—but we decided that, for this idea, it was worth ponying up.

Before we arrived, I designed a visualizer that showed "Twitters"—as we were describing Tweets at the time—drifting through the clouds as if they were birds. We wanted all the Tweets that attendees saw to be about SXSW, but this was before hashtags existed. So we set up a special function. By texting "JoinSXSW" to the number 40404, you opted in to be part of a group of people whose Tweets would appear on the flatscreens.

To make it more interesting, we invited about twelve top geeks, good Twitter users all, to seed the group—people like Robert Scoble, whose blog, *Scobleizer*, was hugely popular with our crowd. When you joined the SXSW group, you were automatically following these ideal Twitter ambassadors. We hoped that when they started using Twitter at the festival, other people in the hall would notice their Twitters on the flatscreens and decide that they wanted to follow them and to watch their own updates appear in the hallways for all to see.

The night before the conference opened, Jack and I had to set up the flatscreens. Our personal laptops were prepped to run the visualizer, and we had to figure out how to connect them so that their displays showed up on the big plasma monitors placed strategically along the hallway. These were mounted on large, moveable audiovisual units. This is an embarrassing confession for a high-tech mogul, but when it comes to hardware—even something as simple as AV equipment—I'm clueless, so this task was far more difficult than it should have been. Do we use "Input 2" or "Input 3"? How do we make it full screen? The resolution was messed up. Also, our Tweets weren't appearing.

By three in the morning we were still working on our displays, and we hadn't had dinner. I had one measly Odwalla bar with me—the gross, green Superfood one. Jack and I split it.

At last we worked out the problem. Our Twitter feed was finally up and running on the first of the eight plasma screens, and we knew what we needed to do to make it work on the rest. We decided to come back to the hall early the next morning to finish setting up.

The next morning, coming off four hours of sleep, Jack and I stumbled back into the hall bright and early, ready to complete the job before the first attendees started arriving. There was just one problem. Twitter was down. Story of our lives.

Twitter had major issues. In those early days, we crashed so constantly that how often we crashed became a joke. There was even a website to deal with the problem: IsTwitter Down.com.

Whatever the problem was this time, there was only one person on the planet who could fix it: an engineer on our team who refused to own a cell phone. And he didn't have a landline, either. We were screwed without him.

Here we were, exhausted, at the end of our ropes, in the middle of a conference hall. There were poster boards on the walls reading, "text 'joinsxsw' to 40404." People were starting to arrive for the first events of the day. We were trying to configure seven flatscreen connections, kneeling behind the units and fiddling with the cords right out in the open. I was wearing the first shirt that I had designed for Twitter. When we launched Twitter, the home page asked, "What are you doing?" So my company T-shirt read, "Wearing my Twitter shirt."

Our engineer was in blissful, phoneless slumber way back in San Francisco, I was wearing my "Wearing my Twitter shirt" shirt, and we looked like idiots.

Eventually, after a nail-biting couple of hours, we were finally online. The display was exactly what we'd planned. The visualizer was the first thing you noticed when you entered the hall. You could tweet, wait a bit, and then see what you wrote float across all of the screens against the backdrop of animated clouds. The folks at SXSW seemed to "get it."

We had accomplished what we came to do. Our ten thousand marketing dollars had been well spent. We could have left then on a high note, but there was more to come.

On the second day of the conference, I was sitting in a lecture about some aspect of technology. It was a packed auditorium, and I was seated at the back. When I glanced around at the open laptops my fellow attendees were holding, I noticed something. Everyone had twitter.com open. They were all using our website! Wow. The flatscreens and the high-profile Tweeters had done the trick. Twitter had taken hold. This was the first sign that we might be on to something big. It would have been enough.

Then, not far into the lecture, people suddenly started getting out of their seats to leave the auditorium. It was as if there had been a loudspeaker announcement telling them to do so. There hadn't been. I checked the time. We still had forty minutes to go. Why was everyone leaving? Had I missed something? It was very strange.

Only later did I find out that the reason everyone had left was...Twitter. There had been no loudspeaker announcement, but there had been a Tweet. Somebody had tweeted that the lecture going on across the hall was amazing. That Tweet was quickly endorsed by several others, in the form of what would later be officially dubbed a "retweet." The information about the better lecture spread so quickly to people's mobile phones and open laptops that the mob decided, almost simultaneously, to leave the discussion in favor of this "must-see" lecture across the hall.

When I heard that story, I was amazed. But it was the next story that really made the hairs on the back of my neck stand up.

That night, there were several parties and lots of packed bars. One person at a particularly crowded pub wanted to hear what his friends and colleagues were working on, but it was just too loud where he was. So this guy sent out a Tweet to his followers suggesting that if anyone wanted to enjoy a quieter conversation, they should meet him over at some other pub that he knew to be pretty empty. He named that pub in his Tweet.

In the eight minutes it took this guy to walk over to the pub he had suggested, hundreds of people had done the same thing, from closer bars. By the time he arrived, the pub was at capacity and there was a long line to get in. His plan had backfired.

What had happened? After this guy sent his Tweet, his followers thought it was a good idea, so they retweeted it to their followers, and so on. This had the snowball effect of creating a real-time swarm of humans—which descended upon this unsuspecting pub in an incredibly short amount of time.

When I heard this story, I thought about a flock of birds flying around an object like a lamppost or a ship's mast. When birds encounter an obstacle, they seem for a few seconds to become one organism. A flock moving as one around an obstacle looks incredibly practiced, almost choreographed. But it's not. The mechanics of flocking are very simple. Each bird watches its neighboring bird's shoulder and simply follows that spot. Twitter was creating the same effect. Simple communication, in real time, had allowed the many to suddenly, for a few seconds, become one. Then, just as quickly, they became individuals again.

———

The people who went to SXSW were the types who were using Twitter actively—so this conference had an unusually high saturation of users for so early in the life of the product. This was the first time we had witnessed Twitter "in the wild." Up until then, it had been just a bunch of our friends goofing around. Those two stories—the massive exodus from the lecture auditorium and the swarming of the bar—flipped a switch in my head and forever changed how I saw Twitter's potential. Now I saw how strangers used the service, and it was a watershed moment.

Flocking, schooling, and a phenomenon called *emergence*— where lots of animals seem to become one "superorganism" far smarter and more capable than any one individual—are common in nature. You see this groupthink in birds, fish, bacteria, and insects. But if you've ever tried to walk through a crowded subway platform or seen footage of Woodstock or flipped on C-SPAN, you know that human beings, as a species, don't naturally flock. Now, for the first time, Twitter, as a new form of communication, was enabling *human* flocking. Twitter was providing an entirely new way for humans to connect. The example that night was only a bunch of people deciding to move to a different party locale—but what if it had been something more important? What if it had been a disaster? What if it had been a righteous cause?

All these thoughts surged through my head when I heard the story about the impromptu pub crawl. Twitter was bigger than we had realized. With all our faults and vulnerabilities, our small team was going to create something that the world didn't know it needed until it had arrived. We had invented a different form of communication, one whose potential was only just beginning to be discovered. If Twitter was to be a triumph, it wasn't going to be a triumph of technology—

it would be a triumph of humanity. I had never thought of technology—or business, in general—in those terms before. Success, I suddenly saw, came from how people used the tools they were given.

———

We were flying high, so to speak, when, at the close of the conference, we went to watch the SXSW Interactive Awards, where various companies were commended for Best in Show, People's Choice, Breakout Trend, and other such categories. Evan, Jack, and I were in the queue to go watch the awards show when a thought occurred to me.

"Wait," I said. "What if we win an award?" For years I'd sat anonymously in the audience during the ceremony, but for the past few days Twitter had been the belle of the ball. There were no nominations for these awards. Who knew what might happen?

"If we win something, we'll have to say something," I said.

Ev said, "You're right. We should have a speech ready in case we end up winning something. Jack should say it. You should write it," he told me.

Write a speech? We were literally standing in the doorway of the awards ceremony. It was impossible.

I thought to myself, *I can't write a legitimately good speech. What can I write in the next three minutes that will come across as clever?*

———

Unlikely as it sounds, I'd been in this situation before. During my senior year of high school, I was in a humanities class.

The classwork was structured around a yearlong project: a major piece of writing on a topic of our choice. As I'll discuss later, I generally made it a policy not to do homework, but an assignment this major had to be completed. The whole grade would be based on this single project, which was due at the end of the year. This was a horrible arrangement for me; I was a major procrastinator.

On the day the project was due, after a year of theoretical work, I had absolutely nothing to turn in. Nada. But I didn't want an F!

I went to class, and while everyone was passing in their papers, I said to my teacher, "I left mine at home on my desk. I can get it now or bring it tomorrow."

She said, "You had a year to do this. If you bring it in tomorrow, I'm going to dock you an entire grade." An A paper would become a B paper.

If I'd done the work, I certainly would have run home to get it. But from an F there was nowhere to go but up. I said, "Fine, if you think that's fair. I'll bring it in tomorrow."

As I've already discussed, constraint breeds creativity. That evening, I thought hard about what I could do in an hour that would seem like it had taken a year. What was physically lightweight, but potentially could look like it had required great time and effort?

Aha! I had it. A play! Plays are made up of dialogue, the epitome of lightweight writing. (Apologies to Chekhov et al.)

That night I wrote a play about two middle-aged guys

playing a basketball game called Around the World. The way
Around the World works is that the players take a series of
shots from a sequence of points on a semicircle on the court.
If you make a shot, you advance to the next point. If you miss
the shot, you have to make a choice. You can stay where you
are, or you can risk taking another shot. If you make that
bonus shot, you advance, but if you miss the bonus shot, you
go all the way back to the beginning.

These two middle-aged guys were friends back in high
school. Now, one of them is the CEO of World Wide Indus-
tries, Inc. He is rich and successful. The other guy has a dead-
end job, painting houses or something. They're shooting the
breeze, talking about their kids, but mostly reminiscing about
high school (which, for me as a senior, fell into the "write
what you know" category).

As they talked and played, the guy who was successful kept
taking the risky bonus shot and advancing around the court.
He was winning the game. The guy who was not successful never moved past the corner. When he missed a shot, he
wouldn't risk the bonus round. At the end of the play, the rich
guy won. He said, "You wanna go again?" That was the end of
the play.

The obvious subtext was that taking risks breeds success.
In those years, I was already forming the philosophies that
would serve me later in life. It was a very entrepreneurial
attitude—I just didn't know it at the time.

I turned my play in the next day. I would have gotten an
A, but it was late, so I got a B. What salvaged my grade was
having the right idea. (Of course, in this case, the severe time

constraints came from my own procrastination, but sometimes, as I've mentioned, constraint can be a motivator.)

What I needed now was the right idea for Jack's would-be acceptance speech, and it came directly from the creativity of constraint.

"I've got it," I exclaimed. "Here's what we'll do..."

It seemed only moments later that Jack, Ev, our good friend Jason Goldman, and I were up on the stage to accept an SXSWi Web Award. Jack went to the podium to accept it. He said, "We'd like to thank you in one hundred forty characters or less. And we just did!"

It was an eighty-character speech, and history was made—in our minds at least.

———

Our team had put many facets of work, inspiration, passion, and creativity into Twitter, but what I saw at SXSW was bigger than the sum of those parts. Once Twitter was available to them, people instinctively knew how to use our service, and as a group, they would guide us. Our jobs, from here on, would be to listen to them, and to build and sustain a service to support their instincts. It was inspiring, and it was humbling.

In the years that followed, there would be Twitter user stories that trumped those of SXSW by many orders of magnitude, but I'll always remember March of 2007 as a major turning point for Twitter and my dreams for what it could be.

———

When we got back from SXSW, Evan, Jack, and I founded Twitter, Inc.

Evan and I went to lunch with our friend from Blogger, Jason Goldman, who had either joined Twitter already or was just about to. Evan wanted some time off. He hadn't taken a break since he'd started Blogger, then Odeo, and now Twitter. What he really wanted was to go be a ski bum for a year. But before he left, he wanted to make sure Twitter's leadership was sorted out so he could chill.

At that lunch, we ate veggie burgers and talked about who should be CEO.

Evan said, "I guess I'll be the interim CEO." It made sense. He was the founder with the biggest financial stake, and he'd been our leader at Odeo. It was a natural assumption.

Still, I said, "If you don't really want to be CEO, you shouldn't be the interim CEO. That's wishy-washy. Why don't we make a decision? Let's make Jack CEO, a real CEO, no interim bullshit."

Goldman disagreed. He thought Ev should be CEO. But Evan didn't really want to at that point.

I advocated for Jack. Jack and I had worked together to create the prototype of Twitter. It was our thing. For part of the time, Noah Glass had come in and taken over. But after working with Noah, Jack had threatened to quit. So Ev had fired Noah and put me back alongside Jack. I never considered taking the role of CEO. I had always thought of myself as a supporting actor. My best gift was helping people.

I said, "Jack's the guy who's writing most of the code. I'm doing all the design work. We're the founders."

Jason said, "Do you think he can do it?"

I said, "It's not like it's General Motors. There are seven of us." All that being CEO meant at that point was signing people's options paperwork, providing some leadership by example, and making sure the work got done.

Though Goldman thought it was a mistake, Evan said, "Okay, you're right. Ask Jack what he thinks."

Back at the office, I went up to Jack. "Hey, Jack, I told Ev you should be the CEO."

Jack spun around in his chair. "Me?"

I said, "Yeah, it was either Evan as the interim CEO or you as the real CEO."

Jack was taken off guard. He didn't initially know if he wanted to do it.

He slept on the idea. The next day, he came in and said, "Sounds great. I'll do it."

We officially spun the company out of Obvious, and Jack became the CEO. I was the creative director. Sometime thereafter, Ev said, "Okay, boys, have fun," and he took off, but he still had the largest stake in the company and was on the board of directors.

In March, before our SXSW launch, we had seven employees and forty-five thousand registered users. By the end of the year, a mere nine months later, we had sixteen employees and 685,000 registered users. At the time, 685,000 was a lot of users, considering how many years it had taken Blogger to get to a million. Now, in the world of hyperconnected news feeds, an app can acquire a million users in a week. But back then you had to claw your way up, literally relying on old-fashioned word of mouth.

———

At SXSW and its breathtaking aftermath, Twitter taught me that our behavior, as humans, is infinitely expandable. The technology of Twitter didn't teach humans to flock. It exposed our latent ability to do so. Mind-blowing! The phenomenon was more than a technology-induced herd mentality. Each of us, each bird, was newly attuned to the birds flying nearby, and to their proximity to other birds. We all were experiencing a view of our place in the world, live and in mid-flight.

6

HAPPILY EVER AFTER

In the spring of 2007, after the South by Southwest conference in Austin, I finally had the sense that the risks I'd taken were worth it. Twitter was going to take off. I was committed to it, and it looked like Livy and I were settled in our little Berkeley house for a while. Then it dawned on me that she and I had been dating for ten years.

It had taken some left turns to find a project I loved, but all the while, there was one emotional investment I'd made in which I never had doubts: Livia.

Back when I was working with Steve Snider at Little, Brown, I wasn't dating anyone. I wasn't even thinking about going on a date. All I was interested in was work. I'd go on long walks and think about stuff. I guess I missed the memo on love. I had my talents, but I could also be completely clueless. One day, Steve Snider and I stopped at a diner on the way in to work. We both looked at the menu, and when the waiter came over, I ordered "Two Eggs Any Style." The waiter was laughing; Steve was laughing; and I was sitting there wondering what everyone thought was so amusing.

Anyway, my friends started staying to me, "You should go on a date, man. You're nineteen years old. You need a girl-friend." Even Steve Snider would say, "You're a young, good-looking guy. You should meet someone."

Everyone was bugging me about it. "Okay," I told them. "I'll go on a date. Next time I meet a nice girl, I'll ask her out."

Not long afterward, I went out to dinner with Steve's family at a restaurant called Paparazzi. (A great name for your restaurant if you want to make sure nobody even the slightest bit famous goes there, ever.) The next day at work, Steve said, "The hostess at the restaurant was pretty. Why don't you go back and ask her on a date?"

I wasn't sure this was a good idea. I was supposed to walk into the restaurant and just ask her out? According to Steve, that was the idea.

"It just seems so…direct," I said.

"This is what people do," Steve said.

So the next day at lunchtime, I went back to Paparazzi. I was sort of hoping the girl wouldn't be there, so I could just tell

Steve that I'd tried and call it a day. But when I walked into the restaurant, there she was. She was fair-haired and nice looking.

But wait—I had no plan. I needed a plan! I walked back out of the restaurant.

I love movies, and back then I particularly loved going to a movie theater called the West Newton Cinema. It had old-fashioned decor and showed art house films. It seemed like a decent place to take a date. I would ask her to see a movie with me at the West Newton Cinema. Okay, I had a plan. I walked back into the restaurant.

"Can I help you?" she asked.

"I was in here a couple nights ago with my boss and his family, and I noticed you, and…do you live in Newton?"

Now she gave me a suspicious look. "Yes," she said. "How did you know that I live in Newton?"

We weren't in Newton. One sentence in, and she thought I was a stalker. Tough start. I briefly considered walking back out of the restaurant.

"Um, I don't know where you live," I explained, "That was a coincidence. I'm trying to ask you go to a movie with me at the West Newton Cinema."

She said, "Oh. Well, I have a boyfriend."

A boyfriend! Of course. Duh. It never occurred to me that this alleged boyfriend might be a made-up, date-avoidance-tactic boyfriend. I was too busy logging the nuances of this unfamiliar new world.

I heard her friend in the background say, "Aw." Aw, as in *Isn't that sweet? This guy actually thought he had a shot with you!*

"Okay," I said. "Thanks for your time."

My first attempt had failed, but instead of being fazed, I was emboldened. *That* was the worst-case scenario? It had been awkward, but it hadn't been so bad. I had a mission now.

Not long after my failed Paparazzi hostess attempt, a young woman who worked in the children's editorial department at Little, Brown walked into Steve's office to drop something off. She was wearing an oversize army coat, and her long dark hair was pulled back. She looked melancholy. I liked her instantly.

She asked Steve to sign something. He did, and she left the office.

I said, "Ooooh." I pointed at the doorway and her receding army jacket. "I think I'm in trouble."

"Her?" Steve said.

"Yeah."

"What about the girl who works in Legal?" Steve asked.

The Photostat machine that we used to reproduce art was in a tiny darkroom with a revolving door that kept the light out. It was so small that there was a sign on the door saying, ONLY ONE PERSON ALLOWED AT A TIME. A few times when I was working in there, the woman Steve was talking about had knocked and come in. She said something like "It's so crowded and dark in here."

I said something like "Yeah, I know. You should leave?" That was me. Totally clueless.

But now I said to Steve, "Who? No, I think I like *her*." The girl in the big army coat.

So I boldly went downstairs to the office that Livia (for that was her name) shared with her boss. I asked her to lunch, and she agreed to join me. But—here's the catch—she insisted on bringing her boss. Let's just say she wasn't optimistic about our prospects.

We set a date, but in the interim, I found an excuse to go back to her office, the way people with intra-office crushes are wont to do. Livia wasn't around, but I noticed that on the computer she shared with her boss, she'd left a sticky note. It read, "Hey, when are you going to fix me up on a date like you promised?"

This was definitely a sign, and it was not a good one. She'd already invited her boss to join us on our date. Now she was actively pursuing other leads. She wanted to date *someone*, just not *me*. Later I would find out that this was because I seemed so sure of myself at work. She figured I'd be overbearing and presumptuous. It's true. I was sure of myself when it came to the work, but I was definitely not confident about going out on a date.

And so we went out to lunch—a cozy, intimate meal at a table for three. To Livia's surprise, I was not a jerk. I was on my best behavior. I was funny and charming and nice. She agreed to go out with me again—this time without her boss. I was really making strides.

Soon enough, Livy and I were dating for real. She came with me when I moved to New York to start Xanga, then to Los Angeles for a stint when I thought I might be a film director, then back to Boston when I sold a book about blogging to a publisher. When I wanted to move west for Google, she thought it was a great opportunity and would be a big adventure. When I decided to quit Google, she supported that, even though we were always worried about money. Livia has always understood what is important to me and has helped me through legitimately hard decisions. Wherever we went, she managed to find a job at a book publisher or a magazine, until she started writing her own books about crafts, such as quilting, ceramics, and stained glass. It's a cliché, I know, but she has stuck by me, and I couldn't have done it without her.

I may have been clueless about dating and relationships, but I didn't let that stop me from taking a shot. What was the worst that could happen? A girl could say that she already had a boyfriend? She could be so uninterested that she'd bring a chaperone on the date? Even if I failed, I'd just be a little less clueless the next time.

When it comes to taking risks, so many of us hedge. It's natural to set up safety nets. I've often met with entrepreneurs who tell me that they are hanging on to their job and tinkering at night on their passion. Of course they are; they need to feed their families. The problem is unless you are willing to accept the worst-case scenario, you can't expect to achieve the best-case scenario. If it is going to reach the potential you dream it will, your true calling needs all your attention. Willingness to take risks is the path to success.

Gattaca is a sci-fi movie about a somewhat dystopian future in which reproductive technology is used by those who can afford it to breed genetically ideal people. Vincent (Ethan Hawke) and Anton (Loren Dean) are brothers, but Vincent was conceived without being selected for superior genetics, while Anton is genetically ideal. Throughout their lives, Anton is better than Vincent at just about everything. A bunch of crazy stuff happens in the movie, but the point is that there's a scene where Vincent challenges Anton to a swim race, a version of "chicken" that they used to play when they were boys. They swim straight out to sea—really far out. The first to give up and turn back to shore loses. Vincent wins. Anton asks Vincent how he beat him. After all, Anton is far stronger and genetically superior. Vincent explains that he gave every ounce of his strength swimming out to sea. He saved nothing for the return trip. This is a revelation for Anton. He is stronger, but he was conservative. He held back instead of giving his all. Vincent, on the other hand, was willing to risk drowning in order to win.

There is a wonderful lesson to be learned from Vincent's decision. In order to succeed spectacularly, you must be ready to fail spectacularly. In other words, you must be willing to die to achieve your goals. Figuratively, of course.

What I'm suggesting is that you embrace the upside of fantastic, epic, earth-shattering, life-changing failure. It's totally worth it if you succeed. And if you fail, you've got a great story to tell—and some experience that gives you a serious edge the next time you go for it. This is a good lesson for startups in general, and for otherwise going for what you truly want. It's like there's a natural force of equality at play. If you really want to succeed big, you have to be willing to risk crazy failure.

It's been widely reported that 90 percent of tech startups fail. Every entrepreneur in any sector is a risk taker. Even some of the most widely known successes had periods of ambiguity or near failure. For example, Pixar began as part of the computer division of Lucasfilm, developing graphics and animation technologies. It hadn't found its footing when Lucas needed money for his divorce and decided to unload it. He sold it to Steve Jobs for $5 million. The animators at Pixar had for a long time wanted to do computer-animated movies, but the costs of making a computer-animated film were too high. Jobs believed in their dream. Twenty years later, Jobs sold Pixar for $7.4 billion.

———

When I was in high school I took a gymnastics class. I wanted to learn to do a back handspring. It's sort of like a backflip, but your hands touch the ground in the middle. I watched other kids do back handsprings and figured the way to do it was to jump backward and land on my hands. But I couldn't seem to jump forcefully enough. I'd chicken out, twist around, and land on my side. I just couldn't do it; I kept falling.

My teacher, seeing my futile attempts, said, "Let me tell you the secret to this maneuver. The secret is that it's easier than it looks. It actually doesn't take that much effort. Here's what you do."

He led me to the mat. "Stand with your arms up, palms up and open."

I raised my hands above my head.

"Now bend as if you're going to sit down, arch your back, and let yourself fall past the point of recovery. Keep your arms outstretched. When you feel your fingers touch the ground, then push with your toes. The key is being willing to fall past the control point. If you can give in to the risk of that, you can perform the back handspring with very little effort."

I did exactly as he instructed me, and it worked. When I went past the point of no return, it was effortless.

The same is true for making a big move in your life. Asking a girl on a date, particularly if she brings a fifth wheel, means you're risking embarrassment and failure. Deciding to quit your job, particularly if it means leaving behind valuable options, means you risk financial ruin and still more failure. But when it works out, isn't it fantastic? When I successfully executed the back handspring, I was in awe. It was all about being willing to fail, just like in *Gattaca*.

———

One of the primary reasons Twitter was constantly breaking was that it was originally built quickly, as one big, messy program. It wasn't a distributed architecture, which meant that it was like a house of cards. If one piece slid out of place, the whole thing fell apart. And each time we wanted to figure out what had gone wrong, we had to sort through the entire system. After hours of forensic study, we'd locate the broken piece and then have to determine who wrote that part of the program. If that person was out sick, tough luck for us. We were disappointing people who used Twitter and getting hammered in the press.

Then one day I was watching an old episode of *Star Trek: Voyager*—"Demon"—when it gave me an idea. The space station is almost out of fuel. The captain orders that they go into "gray mode." Gray mode meant shutting off all nonessential systems in order to use as little power as possible. Essentially, they were putting themselves on life support.

All the systems on the *Voyager* are compartmentalized. They can shut off parts at will, while the ship continues to operate. (I should add that this is kind of an obvious revelation.) The way we built Twitter was not ideal, but it also wasn't a mistake. We weren't planning on the massive success that came in bigger and bigger waves. Nor should we have. It's better to get it built and out in the world than to take years to make it perfect before you know if it's going to work.

I went to work the next day determined to suggest a new approach to Twitter's failures. Jason Goldman had come over from Blogger to be VP of product development and Evan's right-hand man. Luckily for me, Jason was also a *Star Trek* nerd. (The two of us are Trekkies.) I asked him, "Can we make it so that we separate elements of our system into different pieces—like registration, updates, and certain server requests—so that if one piece is going to collapse we can turn off just that section and at least something will work? Then we won't go down completely every time something goes wrong. You can still see the home page. You can still tweet. Could we create a gray mode?"

The answer was yes. That very week, we put together a rudimentary version of compartmentalized features. Now we didn't have to go down completely for every little problem. *Star Trek*: The gift that keeps on giving.

One of Twitter's biggest failures was our so-called platform. In 2007 we released our platform, a collection of APIs (application programming interfaces) that allows third-party developers to make use of Twitter's technology. We loved the idea of inviting developers to build apps that would enhance or complement Twitter, but we didn't think it through enough.

As soon as we released the platform, tons of new Twitter apps sprang into existence. The glut of options muddied the user experience. And allowing all these apps to make essentially unlimited requests to our server hit the service hard. This was a big part of Twitter's stability issues. The developer platform was heavy, expensive, and often contributed to Twitter's breaking down.

When Facebook came out with f8, its platform, I believe it experienced some of the same problems. In the first six months, Catherine Rampell of the *Washington Post* reported, seven thousand new apps had been launched. It was overwhelming, and Facebook had to pull back, most likely by slowly but surely introducing rules and restrictions. Now most of the apps on Facebook are made by Facebook.

Designing book jackets, I had learned that the perfect one satisfies multiple criteria. It pleases Design, Editorial, and Sales. Similarly, a successful software platform should, first and foremost, serve the consumers. Second, it should enrich the developer community so they can make a living while creating fun projects using parts of our code that we'd decided to make public. Finally, it should feed back into the overall value of Twitter, making it a better company and service. Those goals should have determined what we released. Instead, we opened the floodgates. When we had to close some of them later, we upset a lot of people.

We didn't have our eye on the ball. We could have started slowly, releasing specific options for developers to work with that might help make it joyful and easy for users to discover accounts to follow that they wouldn't otherwise have found. But we didn't take a measured, critical approach. The results were damaging for the service, our users, and independent developers. Some failures aren't risks that didn't pan out. Some are just plain old mistakes. All we can do is be honest about them and learn from them.

After SXSW, when I realized Livia and I had been together for so long, I said, "You know what? We should get married."

Livy said, "No shit."

Apparently she'd been hinting at it for a while. She'd say, "Look, they're getting married. They've been dating for less time than we have." Subtle, huh? But I was characteristically clueless.

Nonetheless, emboldened by her promising, albeit obscene, response, I rose to the challenge. After giving a talk at the NASA Ames Research Center, I bought her a cheesy NASA mood ring to serve as a temporary engagement ring.

Livia and I originally intended to elope. We just didn't want the hassle of a wedding and had discovered a beautiful bed-and-breakfast on the coast in Mendocino, California. Somehow, a few dozen friends showed up as our "witnesses," and it turned into something between an elopement and a simple wedding that left out family. This way, we experienced the magic of an easy wedding along with a lifetime of disappointed and angry family members who felt betrayed and abandoned.

Nevertheless, in June 2007, we had a beautiful service in a garden on a bluff above the Pacific. Within a minute of the ceremony, my friend Dunstan snapped a Polaroid photo. It's my favorite picture from the wedding. I'm wearing my linen suit, throwing my head back a bit with a huge smile. My wife is wearing a vintage 1920s evening dress, but we can't see her expression. Her head is down, her face buried in her hands.

While I look like the happiest guy in the world, my wife's body language suggests a woman who has just made the worst mistake of her life. Like she's saying to herself, "What have I done?" Some of the best things in life, I have assured her, come from mistakes. In fact, Ben Franklin once said, "Perhaps the history of the errors of mankind, all things considered, is more valuable and interesting than that of their discoveries."

To this very day, my wife and I remain happily married. As far as I know.

7

ALL HAIL THE FAIL WHALE

Throughout the first years after Twitter exploded at SXSW, the service experienced major connectivity problems. We crashed. A lot.

Companies like to put forward a persona of perfection. "We have the best rates!" "We do the best work!" "We're awesome!" "You should choose us!" "We're world-famous in Poland!" That's normal. But it's also a very safe, contrived path. What if you do fail? Or only sort of succeed? Do you still send out those relentlessly positive messages? You don't want to advertise your failings, but to hide them is, on some level, deceptive. This brings me to the value of vulnerability. When you let people understand that you are people like they are, passionate but imperfect, what you get in return is goodwill.

Take the actor Harrison Ford. (Again, but why not? He's a great actor.) He usually plays the hero. Traditionally, heroes are fearless, strong, and pretty much bulletproof. But Harrison Ford plays it differently. Whenever something really bad is going down and they do a close-up on him, he looks either scared or like he's thinking, *Oh, God, I can't believe I have to do this now.* In *Raiders of the Lost Ark*, faced with a pit of writhing vipers that he has no choice but to pass through, he famously says, "Snakes. Why did it have to be snakes?" There's no bravado. The hero he gives us is a regular guy...and now he's in a snake pit. He'd better figure out how to escape, and fast, if he's going to save his skin. As a viewer, you're far more invested in his survival and success because he lets you see his humanity.

———

For the past decade a large part of my job has been explaining to people why something broke. At Google, when I worked on Blogger in its early days, it broke a lot. I assumed responsibility for explaining to the people using the service what had gone wrong, why it had happened, and what steps we were taking to make sure that particular problem wasn't going to happen again.

One time, in 2003, when Blogger crashed, I set about investigating the cause. Someone finally explained to me that what it came down to was electricity. Google was so huge that it required a vast amount of electricity to support its data centers, the facilities where its computer systems are stored and maintained.

It turned out that when Google ran low on electricity, Blogger wasn't high on the priority list. So we got turned off. I'm simplifying, but that was the basic idea.

When I found this out, I wrote a post on the official Blogger blog explaining that Blogger had gone down because Google was so huge that we'd run out of electricity.

Posting to the company blogs was a big deal, but I always treated it with some irreverence. One of my proudest achievements was that when Blogger launched photos, I used a picture of my cat Brewster as an example. Google was a big, fancy company about to go public, and yet I managed to put a cat picture on its official Google Inc. blog. I wasn't just amusing myself. I saw it as my role to put a human (or cat) face on our technology.

The Brewster post went by without comment, but my post about electricity was a bigger deal. *Where was Google going to get more power?* What I didn't know when I posted about the electricity was that Google had been involved in a secret project. Through a third party, it was acquiring huge swaths of land east of Portland, Oregon, where it planned to create its own power centers. Investors and the media watched the company with hawk eyes. When my post went up, the sleuths of the internet took interest and pieced together what Google was up to. Luckily, I didn't get sent to the principal's office on that one, but sometimes being completely truthful has consequences.

Even so, I believe in honesty, and I believed that explaining mistakes to the people who used our service was the best way to create a long-term relationship with them.

I brought this philosophy to Twitter. At first, I didn't have a master communications plan other than my instincts. I wanted us to let everyone in the company know what we were doing and what we were planning to do. I wanted the external communications to be the same as the internal, minus anything we couldn't legally discuss, or stuff that wasn't classy, such as specific amounts of money raised in financing. I wanted the opposite of a PR team that would spin everything. There should be a universal truth.

Then it became painfully apparent that the service we'd built could not handle its rapidly growing audience. Having made it my job to communicate when things went wrong, I found myself very busy.

I explained any problems to the people using the service (assuming the service was working). If the system crashed, I'd walk down to the engineers to investigate what had happened. Then I'd go on the Twitter blog to report what I'd discovered. Most of the time, I found a way to present it as good news—in the sense that we'd figured out what was wrong and could therefore promise that it was unlikely that particular, exact problem would happen again. (Something else was definitely going to cause the system to crash, but probably not *that*.)

It didn't take long to see the results of my approach. Apple has an annual worldwide developer conference. The first people using Twitter were the same people who were eager to hear about new products and technology Apple might launch, and before the June 2007 conference, there were rumors flying that Apple was going to announce an iPhone.

The day before the conference, all the chatter about the iPhone put a strain on our service. There were intermittent outages, and we—and our users—started to worry that Twitter wouldn't hold up for the announcement the next day.

That night, we stayed late to work on the problems. Our users knew us, and they assumed, correctly, that we had to be killing ourselves trying to bolster the service for the next day. Late at night, a few pizzas arrived, and then a few more. But nobody in the office had ordered pizza.

Then a user tweeted,

Did you get our pizzas?

Oh my God. We were getting support from the Twitter community.

Instead of complaining that the site was down, several different people had sent pizzas over to our office to lift our spirits and support our efforts. We weren't some anonymous robots who frustrated them with our bugs and glitches. All our honesty had revealed our humanity and brought us goodwill.

Twitter continued to fail. It was up to me to decide how to handle this internally, and with our users. I wanted people to know that we were doing our best, but I didn't want to try to hide or downplay our flaws. I decided that we would own our many imperfections.

In an early version of the system, when you sent a text, a "success screen" came up. On most websites, that screen would have read, "Thank you. Your message was sent." On Twitter, our success screen read, "Great, that might have worked."

I'd always wanted to acknowledge the feelings of the person on the other side of the screen. Back at Odeo, when the system crashed, a dialogue box came up where you had to click OK in order to continue. I asked Jack to add a checkbox. Then, in addition to clicking OK you could also put a check next to a line reading: "But I'm not happy about it."

Eventually, in order to soften the blow of Twitter's outages, I poked around on a stock photo website and found an image of a whale being lifted up by a bunch of birds. Perfect! I put it on the Error page.

The Fail Whale, as it came to be called, was a happy, positive image, and it portrayed us as a small but committed group of birds managing, as a team, to carry the weight of an impossibly huge whale. We were small, but we were determined to succeed.

And here's the kicker. There was so much fuss about Twitter's outages that the Fail Whale became a meme. There were fan clubs. There were Fail Whale parties. A guy even got a tattoo of the Fail Whale on his ankle. There was a Fail Whale conference, and I was asked to keynote! People who'd never heard of Twitter started hearing the complaints. What was this service that people liked so much they couldn't bear to live without it? I don't have any scientific evidence, but I believe all the fuss caused more people to check Twitter out. I wouldn't be surprised if the Fail Whale actually contributed to our growth.

Our failures became an asset.

Sometimes we got nasty complaint emails at Twitter. They often said, essentially, "You assholes don't know what you're doing."

My favorite thing to do when I got these mean emails was to respond with kindness in equal amount: "Dear Joe, thank you so much for your feedback. I'm as frustrated as you are when the service goes down. I'm so glad you sent me this note. Here's what the guys are doing. Please let me know if it doesn't work for you in four hours."

Inevitably, I would receive a sheepish, apologetic note saying, "You guys are awesome. I only wrote that email because I really like you."

Receiving these email responses helped me realize that the loudest complainers were often our biggest fans. The only reason they took the time to write was because they had passion for our product. By responding personally and honestly, I was letting them know that we cared, too, and that there were real people behind the scenes doing everything they could to help those poor birds move that whale. It doesn't pay to act bulletproof. Nobody is flawless, and when you act as if you are, it always rings false.

Not only did we encourage angry people to email us, but I put my cell number on the home page of the site and answered the phone when it rang. People would call me for basic support stuff, asking how to log in, how to change an avatar, or whether they could switch usernames but keep their Tweets. One Saturday morning at six o'clock, the phone woke me up. When I rolled over in bed and answered it, an old man's voice said, "Yeah, my church told me we're supposed to use Twitter."

I said, "Okay…"

He said, "So I solved the word puzzle."

This confused me. The day before, I'd had an idea for a multi-player word game that could be played over Twitter. I wanted to call it Wordy. You'd text "play wordy" to 40404, and you'd be given seven letters with which to spell the longest word you could. I'd told Evan the idea the day before, but how did this guy know about it?

"You solved the word puzzle," I repeated.

"Yeah, so now what am I supposed to do?" he said.

Slowly waking up, I realized that he was talking about having filled in the CAPTCHA, the distorted word image you had to match at registration to verify that you weren't a bot.

Caring about our customers meant caring about every single customer's experience, day and night. I explained to the good man how to use Twitter, how to follow people, and how to explore the site.

My contact info was up on our home page until the phone calls were almost exclusively reporters. Then I changed my number.

Over and over again, through the Error messages, the blog postings, the Fail Whale, and responses to user mail, I told people that we were human. We knew we were failing. We didn't like it. But I wanted us as a company to believe what I had seen in *Gattaca*, what I had learned when I took a chance with Livia, and what the success of Twitter would eventually prove to me: Failure was part of the path. It was worth the risk. In fact, it was a critical component of growth. By sharing it with our users, we were showing our ultimate confidence in ourselves and our success. We weren't quitting, and we hoped our faith would inspire theirs.

8

THE BRIGHT SPOT

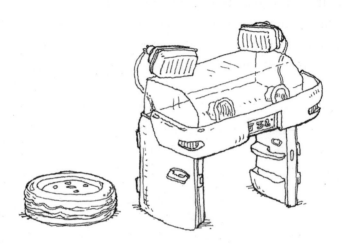

Every company needs an idealist. In general, in the early days of Twitter, my de facto job as co-founder was to be the voice of the company. I spoke to individuals, groups of users, and employees, wrote weekly newsletters to the staff, led Friday afternoon meetings, posted communications through the Twitter blog, and generally kept an upbeat, positive attitude about why we were doing this stuff and why it all mattered. This approach wasn't some kind of master plan. It was just me being communicative.

Nevertheless, it's not fun to fail. People were constantly telling us that the whole concept of Twitter was dumb. Even some of our own engineers had their doubts. On top of that, the service was breaking all the time. This did not feel good. I had helped create Twitter, I was working on it every day, and when it failed, I felt as if I'd done something bad. As if I'd neglected a responsibility. Whenever the app was broken, I was frustrated and on edge until it was fixed.

But lots of times, we didn't know what had gone wrong and it took hours to get ourselves back up and running.

One day, all this stuff caught up with me. Maybe I'd also had a bad commute. Anyway, this time when the service went down, it was the straw that broke the camel's back. I stood up in the middle of our grim South Park office and blurted out something like "This is bullshit. Why can't we get our acts together?"

Jack Dorsey, who was CEO at the time, heard my outburst. He said, "Hey, Biz, will you take a walk with me?"

We walked around South Park, and Jack said, "I need you always to be the guy that has the positive attitude and keeps people feeling like we're on the right track, we're doing good work, and we're happy."

That was the moment when I realized that the company's spirit was one of my key responsibilities. I had often had my own internal struggles, as we all do, worrying that I wasn't helping enough or doing enough work. In the beginning, I was doing all the user interface and design work myself, but by the time of my outburst, we had hired people to handle some of that. I wasn't coding all day long like an engineer.

And I wasn't the CEO. Was I pulling my own weight? Were the things I was doing important? I was giving a voice to the service, I was building a brand, but there was no way to quantify the results of my work.

When Jack told me that he needed me to keep up the company's spirits, I realized that my positivity, though hard to measure, was important. I wasn't just creating a brand for the outside world; I was responsible for the company culture. We hit much lower points with much bigger stakes after that, but never again would I snap as I did that day. I was always able to find the bright spot.

In Steven Johnson's book *Where Good Ideas Come From*, he talks about how good ideas assemble themselves from spare parts we have lying around. As a metaphor, he tells a story set in the Indonesian city of Meulaboh. After the 2004 Indian Ocean tsunami, the hospital in Meulaboh was given eight lifesaving incubators for newborns. What a generous gift! Meulaboh was going to do much better now. But four years later, when Timothy Preston, an MIT professor, checked back to see how the hospital was doing, he found that none of the incubators was working. In the intervening years, they had broken—and nobody knew how to fix them. The expensive, lifesaving technology was useless.

Timothy Preston took particular note of this because he had a team designing an incubator specifically for the developing world. He'd gotten the idea from Jonathan Rosen, a doctor who noticed that in spite of the failing infrastructure in the country, all around were lots of Toyota trucks, and they were running great. So Preston's organization, Design That Matters, built an incubator called the NeoNurture, made of automotive parts. There were headlights for warmth, and the machine was powered by a cigarette lighter or a motorcycle battery. I like to imagine that when Preston delivered the new incubators to the hospital, he said, "Here are some baby incubators. If they break, call the mechanic."

Johnson uses this story to talk about how innovation comes from preexisting ideas "cobbled together with spare parts that happened to be sitting in the garage." But to me it also means something slightly different: finding the bright spot. When everything's wrong and broken, instead of harping on what's wrong and broken, find what works, and build on that. Seek out the positive "bright spot" amid seemingly limitless negativity. Solutions emerge if you look for the positive.

For me this played out in a funny sort of self-fulfilling way. Instead of worrying about what my role was in the company, I let my role evolve to be the not-worrier of the company. But this idea can play out on a larger scale. For example, at the company level, Evan, having given up on podcasting, looked at the Odeo team and decided there was no reason to waste the assembled talent. He may not have thought of it in these terms, but he assumed there was a bright spot, an idea worth pursuing, and he opened the door for it by suggesting the hackathon. In your own company, as Evan did, keep your eyes open for the side project that might deserve center stage. Ten years ago, if you wanted to launch a startup, you had to have a roomful of servers to host the site and its traffic. Since then, Amazon, realizing a side skill it had developed as an online retailer, launched Amazon Web Services, giving even English majors an easy, cheap way to do a startup. Look for bright spots of efficiency—say, a department that fulfills its task so well it might be able to provide that service for other companies—and make space for the skills and interests of your employees and colleagues to thrive.

The same theory applies to even the smallest aspects of life. I'm not saying that if your car breaks down, you can find a way to use it as a refrigerator (though that would be impressive). But say you never find time to clean out the garage. What is it that you always manage to get done? Paying the bills? Then look at why paying the bills happens. Is it because you set aside time for it in your calendar? Do you do a little bit every night? Try applying the same strategies to the garage project.

Beyond the practical, the bright spot theory is about a fundamentally positive outlook. Rose-colored glasses tint the world with false beauty. But an open, curious, optimistic mind yields solutions, and has a better time along the way.

9

BIG CHANGES COME IN SMALL PACKAGES

We came home from South by Southwest in 2007 convinced that Twitter was going to be important. We formed the company. Livy and I got engaged. Free pizzas landed on our desks. That summer, I was dreaming big about the ways people might use the new piece of technology we were creating for them.

One day, when everyone was out at lunch, I started looking through stock photo sites, browsing illustrations—you know,

just for kicks—and I stumbled across some drawings that people were doing with Adobe Illustrator using vector graphics
(images made up of basic geometric elements). It looked easy.
I wanted to try it. *What should I draw? Oh, I'll draw a bird.* So I
drew a bird using Adobe Illustrator. I made it blue. It looked
pretty cool. I gave it a lighter blue tummy, a beak, and some
wings.

When everyone returned to lunch, I showed Ev what I'd
done.

He said, "Oh, that's pretty good."

I said, "Maybe we should put this bird on our site."

Ev said, "Sure." Then he walked away.

So I put the bird up, people liked it, and I started referring
to it as the Twitter bird. A few weeks later I asked my friend
Phil Pascuzzo, a professional designer and illustrator, to give
it a little Phil style. He did a quirkier iteration, and my bird
now had a little hairdo. That was our Twitter bird for a while.
Later, I started thinking more philosophically about it. Any
company could use the first letter of their name as a logo.
Only Twitter could use a bird in flight as a representation of
the freedom of expression. Then I asked our creative director,
Doug Bowman, to make the bird less cartoony, more iconic.
He did a variation on Phil's bird, and I presented it to the
company.

In the presentation, I showed the Apple logo, the Nike logo,
and the Twitter bird. I said to the team, "Guys, in my aspirational vision of the future, people will use Twitter to topple
despotic regimes, and when they do, they will spray-paint
stencils of this bird on the crumbling walls of the tyranny."

Later, Jack asked our art director to have another go at the bird—simplifying it even further—and gave a similar speech.

There were so many ways to get a Tweet onto Twitter that it would be impossible to restrict it. People in any nation would have the freedom to communicate. No matter what the restrictions, people would find a way around them. To shut down Twitter, you'd have to shut down all mobile communications everywhere. We—in the form of our technical weaknesses— were our only obstacle. Twitter was unstoppable.

—

There were only twelve of us goofing around in Twitter's offices on South Park then. I was living in Berkeley and taking the subway home every day. At seven o'clock one evening, I entered the BART station, where I would hop on a train to head under the San Francisco Bay to my house. Just as I boarded the train, I heard some people muttering something about an earthquake.

Whoa! Someone was saying, "Earthquake!" and I was about to go in a giant tube under the bay? That didn't seem like the safest place to be during or just after an earthquake. *Should I dart off the train before the doors close?* I looked around to see if anyone was panicking. It was hard to say. Commuters move around a lot, in all different directions. Was it panic or was it rush hour?

Checking my phone, I saw that I had a bunch of Tweets about the earthquake. One read,

Eh, it was only 4.2 on the Richter scale.

Others reported that it was just a mild earthquake.

Oh, I'll stay then.

Twitter was no longer just an amusement for me, the quirky little app that made me smile. Now it meant the difference between my staying on the train and worrying, or jumping off and being late to get groceries, walk the dog, and see Livy. A small thing—the opinions of a miscellaneous group of people without any authority or expertise in the area of earthquakes. Still, those opinions served a meaningful purpose. Twitter had just saved me a whole bunch of trouble. It was actually making a difference in the way I was living my life.

We didn't set out to build a tool to help people make decisions about earthquakes. This would be our next lesson, the biggest that Twitter had to offer: even the simplest tools can empower people to do great things.

———

Twitter was a small concept, but its growth was exponential. And with that growth came something unexpected. We started seeing the true power of a social network to channel humanity.

In April of 2008, James Buck, a Berkeley graduate student, was in Egypt working on a multimedia project about that country's antigovernment factions. He was following the opposition party, but he was having trouble finding out about their gatherings in time to attend them. Finally, he asked how they were organizing their protests and coordinating the sharing of information. They told him, "We're using Twitter," and introduced him to it (which was kind of ironic, considering he was from the Bay Area).

A week later, James made it to the next spontaneous anti-government protest. Later, when he came to the Twitter offices to tell us about it, he said that police in Egypt tend to have mustaches. It's an unofficial part of the uniform, like for Major League Baseball players here. He said, "When you see a lot of mustaches, you know something's going down."

So he got to the protest, and the mustaches were out in force. James ended up getting arrested with a group of people. For some reason, the police didn't take his phone away. They just threw him in the back of a car. He was really scared— an American kid in Egypt arrested by Egyptian police—and had no idea what to expect. Surreptitiously, in the back of the police car, he tweeted a single word:

Arrested.

His friends back home knew where he was and what he was up to, and they knew he wasn't joking. He could be in serious trouble. They contacted the dean of Berkeley, who arranged for a lawyer in Egypt to help James get out of jail. His next Tweet was again one word:

Freed.

This was good for James, and—now that the concern had passed—a great story for us. We at Twitter, and anyone else who heard the story in the news, could instantly envision infinite scenarios where Twitter could be a lifeline. I was particularly prone to fantasizing about Twitter user stories.

- There's an earthquake. You're trapped under some rubble. Your phone battery is running low. You can text one single friend, or you can tweet a hundred people. Which are you going to do?
- A farmer in India with a crappy phone posts a Tweet asking what a certain grain is trading for at the market fifty miles from his home. The answer is double what he was planning to charge. This changes his life and the life of his family for a year.
- Twitter could be a part of the news, complementary to the Bloomberg News feed. If Bloomberg got three Tweets about something significant from unconnected sources, it could investigate.
- Information could be spread within minutes through retweets. Within one minute, millions of people could be made aware of something important.

The more I imagined the possibilities, the more I saw that the whole value of Twitter was in the way people used it. As a company, instead of talking about how great our technology was (which was tricky to defend, what with the Fail Whale and all), we simply started celebrating the amazing things people were doing with it. It was an odd reversal. Usually companies write press releases about the great stuff they're doing and try to drum up news and interest about it. But we couldn't possibly scour all the Tweets that passed through the system. Instead of telling newspapers what to write about us, we used them to find out the latest lives Twitter had changed, or even saved.

It wasn't about Twitter being brave; it was about brave people doing brave things. But Twitter was a good, trendy hook for reporters. We built a billion-dollar brand because we were lumped in with an ongoing series of incredible human gestures.

We were consistently surprised by the adoption of our service. In short order, all of Congress was on Twitter. *What?* And I never thought celebrities would want to use Twitter. The whole point of being a celebrity is that the public has limited access to you. They have to wait to see you in a movie. *Why would a star want to dilute his exposure by sharing his everyday life?* What I didn't factor in was that celebrities liked circumventing the agents and studios. Twitter was a way they could finally connect directly with fans. I should have known this: just as I had realized that humanizing Twitter would make people like our company, the celebrities wanted to be seen as human, too.

A year after we officially launched Twitter Inc., our office was having startup pains. One problem we had was with the international carriers. In the United States, we'd worked out deals with most of the phone companies. With our short code, 40404, the Tweets people sent were basically free. But in Europe and Canada, we were still paying the bills for every Tweet that went through. One month our bill was six figures! The international carriers hadn't agreed to make the Tweets free.

Our international system was so jury-rigged that it was running from a single laptop. There was a handwritten sign above it reading DO NOT UNPLUG. The sickeningly large bill was my breaking point. When it arrived, I walked over to the laptop and pulled the plug. I unplugged international Twitter. Then I posted to the Twitter blog, essentially saying, "We just turned off all international because it's too expensive." I figured if enough people cared, the carriers would call us to make a deal. Eventually that happened.

The graph of our growth in 2008 looks very steep, and it felt steep to us. But if you look at it in the context of the years that followed, it seems flat—so dramatic was our growth. We weren't yet worried about making money. Our investors understood that something like this had to get very big before it would make money. Evan always said, "There's no such thing as a service with one hundred million active users that doesn't make money. Don't worry."

Meanwhile, our tech was as troubled as ever, breaking constantly—and the faster we grew, the harder it was to keep the service up and running. The company's growth was in spite of itself.

Our popularity lit a fire under the board of directors. Like the rest of us, they wanted Twitter to work. Jack, our CEO, was an engineer. He'd never run a company before. Someone with leadership experience needed to take the reins. So they decided to remove Jack as CEO and put Evan in his place. Needless to say, this caused some bad blood.

When they told me they were going to let Jack go, I pleaded with the board to allow him to stay on for another year to prove himself, but three months later, in October 2008, they yanked him without informing me. I found this out on a Wednesday morning when Evan asked me to meet him at his apartment, two blocks from our office, in half an hour. When I arrived, I found that Ev had also assembled Jason Goldman; our chief technical officer, Greg Pass; and our chief scientist, Abdur Chowdhury. Greg and Abdur had joined Twitter with our July 2008 acquisition of Summize, which gave us the technology to let people search public Tweets. The four of us were probably the last top-level people to hear the news.

We walked to Ev's place. There, Ev said, "The board has decided to remove Jack and replace him with me as CEO." There was a brief moment of silence.

Greg said, "Wow."

I said, "Where's Jack? Does anyone know where he is now?" Wherever Jack was, I was sure he wasn't feeling great. He'd just been kicked out of his own company.

Jack had been getting his marching orders from the board at the same time as Evan told us what was happening. I immediately texted Jack, and he and I met up for lunch right after I left Ev's place. Jack was dejected. He would later describe feeling like he'd been punched in the stomach. I suggested that he break the news to the rest of the team, giving a classy speech wherein he praised the board's decision, told the team that he was taking a higher-level backseat position as chairman of the board, and showed confidence in the company's future success.

Jack ate some soup. Then he said, "I'm going to be like Steve Jobs. I'm going to come back one day." When he said that, his posture changed, as if remembering that Steve Jobs had also been pushed out of his own company made today easier to bear.

As I'd done at SXSW, I wrote Jack a short, classy speech (which included a whole section about how I was charming, funny, and good-looking). This one praised the team and was generally positive, even though he was feeling not so positive.

The truth is that the ghost of Ev as CEO had been there all along. Most of the team had come over from Odeo, where he'd been our CEO. In my weekly internal emails, I often referred to Jack as our "fearless leader," trying to bolster his image. Now I needed to steer the ship back toward Evan.

After he left, Jack and I noodled over an idea for an iPhone app that would help people keep a diary. We met at night at wine bars and worked on it for fun, to fire up our brains, and to have a reason to continue working together. Then Jack disappeared for two weeks. When he came back he told me he was working on a new project with a guy named Jim.

"Turns out using the headphone jack in a smartphone, you can read the magnetic strip of a credit card. So you can turn a phone into a credit card reader," he told me.

"Whoa, that's crazy," I said.

That idea was Jack's new startup, Square. I became an angel investor. I knew I wanted to have some level of participation in any project Jack was spearheading.

With the shift in leadership and the tech issues, the team was fractured. We were a laughingstock in the tech world. Programmers were blaming each other. As always, when all else fails, turn to *Star Trek*. There is a *Next Generation* episode called "Attached." It focuses mainly on Captain Picard and Dr. Crusher. In it they're alone on the planet Kesprytt III. Some of its inhabitants capture them and implant them with "transceivers" that allow them to hear each other's thoughts. At one point, while they're walking, they lose their way. Captain Picard says, "This way." But the doctor, reading his mind, says, "You don't really know, do you?" The captain admits that sometimes being a leader means cultivating the appearance of confidence.

That's my leadership move. Saying "This is what we're going to do. This is the right thing," gives everyone the sense of a common mission. We needed to focus on something that felt bigger than our off-balance company. The 2008 presidential election was on the horizon, and both candidates had Twitter accounts. Election Night was going to be important for Twitter. Yes, it was a historic election, and sure, the results would determine the course of our country. But all I was focused on was (a) whether Twitter would stay up and running and (b) how we could use this big event to resurrect our team morale. To make us feel team-y again.

———

In the months leading up to the election, we all worked hard, as a team, to fix the capacity problems that had plagued us.

The candidates may have thought it was their show, but like

a news team, we felt it was ours. And I have to say, it worked. The team came together.

The week of the election was a big week for Twitter, not to mention for the United States, and the world. I sent the team a rallying email with the header: "Adding a New Feature to Democratization of Information." It read:

Folks,

Birds in flight have an amazing ability to move as one—immediate feedback and simple rules create something grace-fully fluid and seemingly choreographed. In the spring of 2007, we caught a glimpse of people harnessing a similar power for a new kind communication. South by Southwest 2007 intro-duced us to the incredible relevance of Twitter during a shared event.

Now the world is watching as one of the most massively shared events in US history unfolds before us. Twitter is posi-tioned to support this election process like nothing else before—37 members of Congress are Twittering, both candidates have active accounts, millions of citizens are reacting to issues in real time, and political activists are organizing protests—all using Twitter, all moving as one.

Okay, it was a little over the top. But when I wrote that note to the Twitter team, I wanted them to come away from it thinking, *Holy shit, my work is important!* I wanted them to share the email with their husbands or wives, saying, *Look! What I'm doing matters.*

A crew of us stayed late on Tuesday, Election Night, to make sure everything was running smoothly. We invited about fifty people to join us for food and drinks, and watched the election results on the big screen. What happened next was amazing. Twitter exceeded and sustained normal capacity by 500 percent—without breaking a sweat.

The servers stayed up. And we had our first African American president! That was the order of the news in our offices that night. Call us Ishmael—our whale was, for the moment, nowhere to be seen. And with the great beast safely out of sight, we welcomed the first U.S. president to have an official Twitter account.

———

A few weeks later, there was a series of terrorist attacks in Mumbai, India. People in the middle of the crisis used Twitter to report what was happening in real time, and in some cases Twitter served as a lifeline.

People everywhere were finding the reasons Twitter was relevant in their lives—from reading movie reviews to helping the homeless to spontaneously raising money for world causes. While we were buckled down, focusing on performance, the rest of the world was figuring out what Twitter was for.

I wasn't the only person having big ideas about how Twitter could be used. On July 30, 2008, a 5.4-magnitude earthquake hit Southern California. The official time of the quake was 11:42 a.m., but the Tweets announcing it came in earlier than that. Nine minutes later, at 11:51, the Associated Press sent out a fifty-seven-word alert on its wire service. In those nine minutes, Twitter saw thirty-six hundred Tweets with the word *quake* in them. In that nine-minute news gap, we had assembled an entire book's worth of firsthand accounts of the event. Of course Twitter isn't a traditional news service. Our reports don't disseminate reliable data and facts. They're user generated and 140 characters or less. What Twitter has to offer is speed. The AP is as fast as it can be. But Twitter has a global user base sending messages every second, in real time. Whether or not it's the future of news, it's at least complementary. Getting information quickly is one of the best things you can do on the planet. Twitter instantly connects us to what is happening in the world.

In the Bay Area, everything always comes back to earthquakes and how best to endure them. That July 30, people were tweeting as they were experiencing the earthquake; they couldn't resist. The impulse to tweet, mid-quake, was too strong. Those Tweets created a map measuring the impact and reach of the event. And the Tweets spread faster than the quake. Twitter could beat earthquakes to the punch.

Wait a minute. This thing isn't just for breakfast anymore. It's not just for reporting what's happened. It's able to predict what's gonna happen. Experts in the emergency response field saw immediately that Twitter could do something that their systems couldn't. They started calling us, wanting to work with us to make Twitter an official part of the emergency response service, but I told them it was too early. Our service wasn't reliable enough yet. We didn't want someone to die because Twitter had gone down.

Nonetheless, after that earthquake, we, and the world,

saw Twitter's potential in an even greater light than before. In order to realize that potential, we needed to be both ubiquitous and reliable. We were charging ahead on both fronts.

———

In January of 2009 we were in our Bryant Street offices, the place we'd moved to after the funky office on South Park, and were in the middle of what we call Tea Time, a weekly all-hands meeting. Tea Time is a take on Google's tradition of TGIF, in which every Friday they had free beer and snacks. Jack likes tea, so he thought that, instead, we could meet, talk about the week's achievements, and enjoy tea and crackers together. But as soon as people realized there was beer in the fridge, there was no turning back. That particular day, we were hosting a *Wired* reporter, who was spending the week with us for an article about Twitter. He was sitting discreetly in the corner, not looking to report the specifics of the meeting but getting a general sense of what it was like at Twitter. Then he spoke up.

"Hey guys, I don't want to interrupt, but a plane just crash-landed in the Hudson River. A guy on the ferry that's helping with the rescue took a picture with his iPhone and tweeted it."

The meeting broke up. We all went over to look at his computer. It was a perfect picture, showing people in business suits standing on the wing of a US Airways plane in the middle of the Hudson.

The 2008 election had been the definitive moment for us because we'd pushed the technology to a new capacity. But this was a definitive moment for the role of Twitter in the realm of messaging. We all have many different options for contacting people electronically: email, text, IMs, Tweets. There is a time and a place for each. When a plane lands in the Hudson in front of you, that's a Tweet. That's the ultimate Tweet. You don't email a friend that. You tweet it.

On April 7, 2009, I came into work to find my in-box full. My office phone was loaded with messages. It was the press, and they were all asking the same question: What was Twitter's role in today's student riots in Moldova?

Um...where?

I wanted to write back saying, "Well, we didn't like what was going on in Moldova, so we pushed the big red Moldova button here on our wall at Twitter and triggered the revolt."

Instead, I looked up Moldova on Wikipedia. It turned out that students in the country between Romania and Ukraine— I knew those two—had organized to protest Moldova's preliminary election results, suspecting that they were fraudulent. Because they had used Twitter to organize, the media were calling it the Twitter Revolution.

The user stories I'd envisioned were all coming true, and more so. All of this from an app that began with Jack and me sharing what we were having for breakfast. I no longer had to tell our employees that what they were doing was important. It was clear.

As I explained in an article in the *Atlantic* on October 19, 2010, there was of course some backlash against the idea of Twitter changing the world. In the *New Yorker*, Malcolm

Gladwell wrote, "Some of this grandiosity is to be expected. Innovators tend to be solipsists. They often want to cram every stray fact and experience into their new model." This bugged me because we weren't the ones taking credit for the Moldova protests. On the contrary, we'd been going out of our way to make it clear that we *didn't* think Twitter was the voice of revolution. Twitter was just a tool that people were using to do great things. And wasn't that amazing enough? *If you give them the right tools, people do great things.* Nobody said that the telephone brought down the Berlin Wall, but were phone calls made? Hell yeah! Twitter was proof that leaderless self-organizing systems could be true agents of change.

As the Arab Spring began at the end of 2010, it became even more important for me to clarify Twitter's role.

Activists in Arab countries used Twitter and other services like Facebook to organize uprisings. It got so that we could practically predict the next revolution. We'd start to see mounting Tweets in a certain area and we could have made a phone call, "Hey, dictator, you might want to flee."

Suddenly, as the Arab Spring progressed, every major news outlet wanted me to come on and talk about what was happening. My instinct was not to do that. Not just because I was afraid of being outed as an idiot when it came to global affairs, but I felt that it wasn't right to gloat—or even focus on what all this meant for our business. People were dying. I wasn't going to go on TV and say, "Yeah, look at us! We're a great company!"

While we were glad to be a visible part of the changes taking place, I wanted to be very careful about what our role was. We didn't have a publicist or anything, so I was the de facto guy deciding if we'd talk to members of the press and about what. So I decided not to talk to any of them. Some of our board members and closest investors were kinda like, "What? Are you crazy? This is huge international news exposure." They had a point—whenever we went on TV, a million new people signed up to Twitter—but I still wanted to say no to all the major media outlets. I didn't want to piss them off. I hoped they would talk about Twitter at some point; I just couldn't endorse it under those circumstances. So I wrote to Raymond Nasr, my friend and communications adviser. I forwarded him the email I wanted to send in response to the media requests. It was short, and it basically said, "Thank you for your interest, but we're not talking about this." Raymond, who has always had a great economy of language, said, "It's perfect. I'd just add the word *inappropriate*."

So I sent out an email saying, "Thanks so much for the opportunity, but we don't think it would be appropriate for us to do the interview or to offer comments beyond what we've already addressed to the public on our company blog."

Most of the responses I received read, "Understood."

When I wanted to get the job at Blogger, I'd visualized myself working there. I believed that kind of visualization had the power to make things happen. Now, as the user cases I'd envisioned for Twitter all came true, it felt like a waking dream.

Things had gotten very serious very quickly. Suddenly we had to make choices about how we interacted with governments.

Occasionally we needed to take down the service for maintenance. Whenever we did that, we put up a note warning the users. But in June 2009, when we put up our customary maintenance notice, we immediately got about a hundred calls and emails saying, "You can't take the service down then! There's a scheduled demonstration in Iran." The Iranian government had shut down other means of communication, and Twitter was considered vital.

Among all the emails we received during that incident, one message stood out. It came from one of our board members. A U.S. government employee had sent a note to him, and he forwarded it as an FYI.

The State Department didn't want Twitter to go down for maintenance.

Jason Goldman and I hashed out the decision. We needed to do this maintenance—we'd already postponed it thirteen times, and if we didn't do it soon, the system would possibly break forever.

Finally I said, "Let's move the maintenance one more time." It wasn't because I wanted to follow the State Department's orders—I didn't pretend to understand the situation—but because Twitter was *supposed* to work, and our job was to keep it up and running. What was happening in Iran was directly tied to the growing global significance of Twitter and its importance as a communication and information network.

So we rescheduled the planned maintenance for midafternoon, which was the middle of the night in Iran. To an outside observer, it may have looked as if the State Department had made a call on their red phone and we scrambled to make the change. The thinking was: If we postponed maintenance because the U.S. government had asked us to, then what else were we supposed do for them? But the government did not have decision-making power at Twitter. We didn't want to help our government, or any other government. We had to stay a neutral technology provider.

On June 16, 2009, the day after the maintenance, I posted the following message to the Twitter blog:

> Twitter is back and our network capacity is now significantly increased. The planned maintenance that we moved from last night to this afternoon was a success and it took half the time we expected.
>
> When we worked with our network provider yesterday to reschedule this planned maintenance, we did so because events in Iran were tied directly to the growing significance of Twitter as an important communication and information network. Although presumed impossible if not extremely difficult, we decided together to move the date. It made sense for Twitter and for NTT America to keep services active during this highly visible global event.
>
> It's humbling to think that our two-year-old company could be playing such a globally meaningful role that state officials find their way toward highlighting our significance. However, it's important to note that the State Department does not have access to our decision mak-

ing process. Nevertheless, we can both agree that the open exchange of information is a positive force in the world.

Our stance was that we were government-neutral. We were a communications tool. We didn't help any state, whether for the sake of revolution or the aid of government investigations. I was proud when, exactly four years later, on June 7, 2013, Claire Cain Miller wrote an article in the *New York Times* titled, TECH COMPANIES CONCEDE TO SURVEILLANCE PROGRAM, about PRISM—the U.S. government's secret surveillance program— and said that when the National Security Agency came to Silicon Valley companies asking for user data, "Twitter declined to make it easier for the government."

Alexander Macgillivray, our general counsel—whom everyone called Amac—had done everything he could to legally support our stance. We weren't in service to any government, and we made any government attempts to access our user information a huge pain in the ass.

We tried to keep our goal pure: to connect people everywhere instantly to what was most meaningful to them. For this to happen, freedom of expression was essential. Some Tweets might facilitate positive change in a repressed country, some might make us laugh, some might make us think, some might downright anger a vast majority of users. We didn't always agree with the things people chose to tweet, but we kept the information flowing irrespective of any view we might have about the content.

We believed that the open exchange of information would

have a positive global impact. This was both a practical and an ethical belief. On a practical level, we simply couldn't review all one-hundred-million-plus Tweets created and subsequently delivered every day. From an ethical perspective, almost every country in the world is in agreement that freedom of expression is a human right.

We had come a long way from being labeled the *Seinfeld* of the internet. We were on our way to becoming a grown-up company putting out a small, simple tool that could be harnessed for big change. We hadn't changed the world, but we'd done something even more profound and had learned a deeply inspiring lesson: When you hand good people possibility, they do great things. There's no such thing as a superhero, but together we can spin the world in a new direction.

10

FIVE HUNDRED MILLION DOLLARS

Twitter had captured the attention of the world. On a Monday in late 2008, not long after Evan took over from Jack as CEO, I woke up in my little house in Berkeley and, for some strange reason, decided to wear a dry-cleaned, pressed white shirt that day. I never wear a shirt like that, but I saw it in my closet and put it on, and Livia said I should wear it. So I did.

I walked the thirty minutes it took to get from our house

to the downtown Berkeley BART station, swiped my card through the turnstile, sat down on a bench, and waited for the train. It takes twenty-three minutes to get from downtown Berkeley to the Montgomery Street station in San Francisco, and the train, as I've mentioned, travels in a tube strapped to the bottom of the San Francisco Bay. It always makes me a bit nervous, which made my questionable white shirt a bit sweaty. I knew that shirt was a mistake.

Carrying my PowerBook on my shoulder, I walked the thirty minutes it took to get from Montgomery Station to our office on Bryant Street. By the time I got into the office, approximately two hours after waking up, I was shvitzing a bit.

As soon as I walked into the office, Jason Goldman told me that Ev, who had recently taken over from Jack as CEO, was waiting for me in his car downstairs.

It wasn't normal for me to show up at work and be told that Ev was waiting for me to go to a meeting. Something was up.

"Why's he waiting for me? What's the meeting?" I asked.

"Just go."

So I turned around and went back outside the building. Indeed, Ev was waiting for me in his Porsche.

I got into the car. "Where are we going?"

"Palo Alto."

"Oh! Is today the day we're supposed to do that Q-and-A at Google?" I said. "I wish I hadn't worn this shirt. I feel weird in this shirt." It was just an ordinary white button-down shirt, like a suit shirt, but I was obsessing. Should I have tucked it in? I already felt awkward in the stupid shirt, and now we were going to Google.

We started driving toward 101 South. Ev likes to drive fast. And in spite of his general patience with me, he gets annoyed when I babble without thinking.

"Stop talking," he said. "We're not going to Google. We're going to Facebook."

"Why are we going to Facebook?"

"To see Mark Zuckerberg."

"Why?" By this time we were racing down 101.

"Facebook wants to acquire us." Sometimes Evan is an enigma. When he said this, his expression didn't change at all.

"Oh," I said. "Do we want to be acquired?"

"I don't know. Probably not."

We didn't speak for a few minutes, while Ev dodged and passed cars, maneuvering in and out of the fast lane. I thought about our last round of financing. It had placed the company's valuation at something like twenty-five million dollars.

"How much does Facebook want to acquire us for?" I asked

"I don't know."

"Do you want to sell the company to Facebook?" I asked again.

This time Ev said no.

"Well," I said, "why are we going down to Facebook, then? I feel weird in this shirt."

Ev said the shirt was actually appropriate for the trip—I could tell he was trying to end the shirt part of the conversation—and that it was too late to back out now. He had agreed that we would meet Mark Zuckerberg and talk about acquisition.

"If we don't want to sell the company," I said, "maybe we should just make up a price so ridiculous that nobody would ever pay. That way, we honor the obligation of having the conversation but we get out of it."

"What would be a crazy number?" Ev asked.

I blurted out the biggest number I could possibly imagine: "Five hundred million dollars." I started laughing before I was even finished saying it. Ev started laughing, too. We were speeding down 101 laughing out loud imagining how funny it would be if Mark Zuckerberg asked us how much we would sell the company for and we said five hundred million dollars. We laughed for a few minutes. Then Ev said it probably wouldn't be as simple as that. It was unlikely that we would actually talk numbers.

Arriving in Palo Alto, we parked the car at a meter. Facebook didn't have a big campus yet. Its headquarters were spread across a few office buildings in downtown Palo Alto. We walked to the address. A receptionist gave us nametags and told us we should wear them so that the staff knew we were visitors. We dutifully stuck them on our shirts.

After a few minutes, one of Mark's trusted lieutenants greeted us. He led us past some folks who were coding away at computers and to a modest office where Mark was sitting at his desk. As we approached, Mark stood up to shake our hands. We did the usual hellos.

"You guys didn't need to wear nametags," he said.

Ev responded. "Yes, we did. The woman at the front said so."

"Yes, she did." I backed Ev up.

Mark asked us if we wanted him to show us around. We said sure, so he walked us back the way we had come in. As we followed, he gestured toward a bunch of people working at computers, saying something like "Here are some of our people working." Indeed.

He took us to the elevators and showed us a wall that had been decorated with graffiti. He said, "This is our graffiti wall." It sure was. We said it was pretty cool.

The elevator took us to the ground floor, and Mark asked if we wanted to see another building. Ev and I exchanged a glance—in one look, we said to each other, "This is awkward but I guess we'll go with it."

So Ev said, "Yeah, sure, we'll check it out."

Since the buildings were spread around a few blocks of downtown Palo Alto, we found ourselves walking down the sidewalk, me in my uncomfortable white shirt, both of us sporting nametags, trailing after Mark Zuckerberg.

Again, awkward.

We arrived at another building and entered. Mark took us upstairs and showed us some more people working at desks. As we walked by them, Mark said something like "Here are some more people working."

Yup. He was right. There were more people working, just like in the other building. I gave Ev a "what the hell?" look, and he stifled a laugh.

Mark suggested we talk and led us to a small room on the other side of the floor that was probably an unoccupied office. The room was just big enough for one chair and one love seat. Mark walked in first and took the chair. I walked in next and squeezed onto one side of the cozy love seat.

Coming in last, Ev said, "Would you like the door open or closed?"

Mark's response was "Yes."

Yes, what? The answer didn't compute. Ev paused for a second, waiting for Mark to correct his answer, but no further instructions were forthcoming, so he said, "I'll just close it halfway," and carefully adjusted the door to a slightly ajar position.

All these things: my white shirt, the nametag issue, the tour of nothing, the door positioning, the tiny love seat where Ev wedged himself next to me (it's a good thing he's so skinny), the people sitting right outside the random office listening in on whatever we said—these things and more made the whole situation extremely uncomfortable.

I started us off saying something like "Mark, I want to tell you I admire what you're doing. And I think we're doing the same work. We're both democratizing information, and I love it."

Mark just looked at me with an expression that said *I'll wait for the clown in the white shirt to finish so I can talk to the smart guy.* What can I say? I'm a talker. Sometimes Ev has to say, "Okay, Biz, can you stop talking now, please?" Even when it's just the two of us meeting, occasionally Ev will say, "Biz, can I talk now?"

Mark quickly got down to business. He said, "When it comes to partnerships, I don't like to talk about numbers."

"Neither do we," Ev said quickly.

"But," Mark added, "if you were to say a number, then I could tell you yes or no right now."

What were we supposed to do? After hemming and hawing a bit, Ev just went for it. He said, "Five hundred million dollars."

Wow, I thought. *He actually said that number.* As I've mentioned, Evan is a very grounded individual. He likes building productivity applications that help you make to-do lists and check them off. All his time is accounted for. Later he would even use his calendar to set aside time to play with his children. I was pretty sure "Offer our company to the founder and CEO of Facebook for five hundred million dollars" was not on Evan's to-do list. I looked at Evan, but he was focused on Mark.

There was a slight pause, and then Mark said, "That's a big number."

That was my cue to make an inappropriate joke, so I jumped in: "You said you would say yes or no, but instead you said, 'That's a big number.'"

Ev laughed, but Mark didn't. Okay, this was not my meeting. Blame the shirt.

Instead, Mark said, "You guys want to have lunch?"

We agreed and followed Mark out of the building to yet another nondescript building in Palo Alto. This housed the Facebook cafeteria. It had a long line out the door and around the block. (Free armchair-CEO tip to Facebook: fewer graffiti walls, more food service staff.) Now it was Ev's turn to attempt a bit of humor.

"Aren't you the boss? Can't you just cut to the front of the lunch line?" he joked.

"That's not how we do things here." Then he turned his back to us and we started waiting. Mark had thought Ev was serious. We were as alien to him as he was to us.

I'm pretty sure both Ev and I were visualizing the same thing: a long, silent wait in line for our food followed by an even more awkward high school–style lunch during which Mark would continue to point things out to us: "Here are some people eating," or "Here are some people wondering why we don't have more food service staff." So I pulled the old line: "Oh my gosh, Ev. We have that *thing*."

"Oh yeah, the *thing*." Ev said. Because a friend knows what it means when a friend has a *thing*.

"We have a thing back up in the city," I said to Mark. Maybe he believed me and maybe he didn't, but since we obviously spoke a different language, it was impossible to guess how he took it. We left anyway. "Here are some people leaving."

Taking that meeting was a rookie mistake. If you're not serious about selling, you shouldn't take an acquisition meeting, because once an offer is made, you have an obligation to present it to the shareholders for serious consideration. There are three reasons an entrepreneur sells his company, and none of them applied to us. One, you're about to be crushed by competition or sued into oblivion. Two, you're tired or done and just want the money already. Three, your company's potential, when paired with another company, is orders of magnitude bigger than you can possibly imagine attaining alone. (Actually, at the time, Twitter was doing so miserably, technically speaking, that we almost fell into the category of entrepreneurs who should sell because they're just about screwed. It might have been a good idea to go to Facebook, but we weren't ready.)

Unbelievably, within the week, Mark Zuckerberg came to us with an offer. It was a mix of cash and stock that added up to, drumroll please...*five hundred million dollars*. That number had come out of nowhere. It was simply the biggest number I could think of. I didn't even know if there was that much money in the world. It had started as a joke, and now it was real. Talk about creating your own opportunities.

The offer was a big shocker, and a banner day for Twitter. We had a call with the board to discuss what to do, and then Evan composed a very convincing letter to the board explaining why we weren't ready to sell. All signs pointed to Twitter's potential to succeed. We had barely gotten started. We thought we could build a business, but the only way to find out was if we went for it.

The truth of the matter was that we were as passionate about Twitter as we had been from the start. We wanted to see it through. We were playing by our own rules, and we were willing to bear the consequences if it all came crashing down.

Again, the takeaway here isn't about my behavior, which I'm the first to admit was juvenile bordering on obnoxious. Making jokes about massive amounts of money and then proposing them to serious potential investors is no way to build a career or a business. The point is to trust your instincts, even if you're smaller and less powerful than the other guy.

Several months later, in a round of financing led by Benchmark Capital and Institutional Venture Partners, Twitter was valued at two hundred fifty million dollars. Facebook's offer, based on my joke, had spiked our value. Who knew that this was how these things worked? I had assumed a lot more went into the valuation of a company, but as it turns out, it's not much of a science. It starts at zero, and then one day you find yourself in a room telling people they can have x percent of your semi-existent company for x million dollars. You set your company's own valuation. It's made up, and then it's affirmed by what people are willing to invest. .

These days Twitter is worth something like fifteen billion dollars. One day it could be worth a hundred billion. Those, Mr. Zuckerberg, are really, really big numbers.

Nowadays I co-teach an MBA class at Stanford with one of the partners from Benchmark. The focal point for the year is this question: Should Benchmark have invested in Twitter at the level it did when it did it? The students research the company, the market, the competition, and other factors in valuation. A chief point in their research is the five-hundred-million-dollar Facebook offer, which helped set the price. It always amuses me to get up in front of the class, to look at all the serious, hardworking MBA students, and to say, "Do you guys know that it was a joke? A crazy joke?"

Four years later, in 2013, Facebook bought Instagram for one billion dollars in cash and stock. A billion dollars! Driving to Palo Alto in Evan's Porsche, I couldn't even conceive of a number that high. I like to think that Mark Zuckerberg learned something from his encounter with us. He wasn't going to hedge his bets this time with some paltry offer like five hundred million in a mix of stock and cash. He probably said to Kevin Systrom, the creator of Instagram, "You've been working on this for eighteen months. I will give you one billion dollars." I mean, startup, schmart-up. Who could say no to that?

11

WISDOM OF THE MASSES

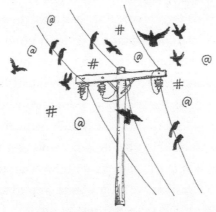

As far back as 2007 people had started calling the updates to Twitter *Tweets*, and called the action of posting an update *tweeting*. In early news articles, the grammar police took note of this evolution. I loved it. In-house and publicly, we were just calling them updates, and called the act *twittering*.

The Twitter sidebar displayed your usage statistics, including the number of updates you'd made. Jason Goldman and I had a conversation about whether to change this to count user *Tweets* instead of *Updates*. I didn't want to endorse the user-generated terminology right away. Having the users take ownership of the nomenclature was fantastic. It was like how *Google* became a verb. But I was afraid that if we, the company, started calling them *Tweets*, for users it would be like having their parents say that something was cool. I didn't want to mess with the magic. So we held off using the *Tweet* terminology publicly or changing *Updates* on the site to *Tweets*. When asked what the terminology was, I'd say, "The service is called Twitter, and the act of using it is called twittering." (That nearly screwed us later, when we tried to copyright the word *tweet*, because there was little evidence that we as a company had been using it.) Finally, in the summer of 2009, when the word *Tweet* was so widely adopted that *Update* sounded too generic, we went through and changed the terminology on the site. I was thrilled.

When it came to listening to the folks who used Twitter, we put our money where our mouths were. Watching for patterns of use across the system, we built features based on those patterns. Larry Wall, who created the programming language Perl, once said, "When they first built the University of California at Irvine they just put the buildings in. They did not put any sidewalks; they just planted grass. The next year, they came back and put the sidewalks where the trails were in the grass. Perl is just that kind of language. It is not designed from first principles. Perl is those sidewalks in the grass." Hashtags, @replies, and retweets emerged in just that way.

Shortly before we went to SXSW in 2007, a guy named Chris Messina, a friend, who at the time was running an internet consulting firm called Citizen Agency and was an early Twitter adopter, walked into our office. I was in the middle of eating a really great taco. Chris said, "You should make it a feature that if someone types #sxsw that means they're twittering about South by Southwest."

Jason Goldman and I listened to Chris's idea politely but secretly thought it was too nerdy to catch on. Sure enough—maybe Chris started it—people soon began using hashtags. They were using them for about a year when, in July 2009, we decided to hyperlink the hashtag term automatically to the Twitter search results page for that term. Now when you clicked on #sxsw, for example, you were given a page showing all the search results with that same hashtag. It was fairly simple to do, so even though we weren't sure people would use it, there was no harm in trying it out. It seemed like a good enough way to group search results. Nowadays hashtags are so common that they're used ironically, in contexts that have nothing to do with Twitter or linking subject matter.

Tweeters also came up with their own method for directing their messages to a specific person, by using the @ symbol. Starting your Tweet with @biz, for example, means you are talking to me specifically, much as you might single out a particular person in a group conversation. Back in 2007 we started supporting this behavior by doing things like linking the "@username" to a profile, then later to a given conversation. This use of the @ symbol was not a new thing on the web. It was used in early online chat forums in order to refer to someone who said something earlier in the thread. You'd type, "I agree with what @hamguy44 said."

As the use of the @ symbol evolved, we updated the site. People started using the symbol not just to talk to a specific person, but to reference something, as in

I rode @BART to work.

In 2009 we started referring to @ replies as "mentions," and collected them on profile pages so a person (or BART) could easily see all the places where he, she, or it had been mentioned. Later we collected them so that people could follow a conversation on Twitter.

Retweeting was a little more controversial. We noticed that when someone liked a Tweet, she would copy and paste it into her Twitter field. When she tried to credit the author, she'd exceed the character count, so she'd have to abridge the original Tweet. Then she'd add "RT" to indicate that it was a retweet.

We said, okay, this is a useful feature, because if a Tweet is good and people want to retweet it, a good idea could spread. But we should make a button that retweets the original in such a way that you can't modify it. That way, people won't be misquoted. The Tweet will be posted on your behalf in its pure form. Also, because it will be a button, it will be easier than cut-and-paste, which is so clunky. Popular Tweets will spread really fast. So if there's a particularly good Tweet from a guy who has seventeen followers, and I retweet to my two hundred with the click of a button, the Tweet will spread like wildfire.

Making retweeting into a one-click action was useful to us because it was trackable. If something was retweeted a lot, this signaled to us that it was interesting or important. We could use retweeting to pull hot topics to the surface. We would eventually create an area called "Discover" that, among other things, highlighted the most retweeted Tweets.

Initially people were annoyed. They didn't like the fact that you couldn't edit a retweet. They were used to controlling it and didn't want that to change. But we held strong. Sometimes people resist change. Our way preserved the integrity of the original Tweet, and it allowed us and users to trace its path, and know for sure exactly who said what. Nobody could fake retweets from other people. This is an example of how we listened to our users but also considered what we believed made the most sense for the community and the service, confident that even the detractors would soon see that.

This is true emergence, the wisdom of crowds—like flocking, it represents group members making choices together. The bigger message of the nomenclature evolution was exactly what I had been telling new Twitter employees. It was our job to pay attention, to look for patterns, and to be open to the idea that we didn't have all the answers.

The reason this approach to business is unorthodox is that in many traditional forums, you simply can't have such direct contact with your users. If you're a basketball manufacturer, you can't see all your customers bouncing the balls. But we could see the Tweets. It was impossible not to. We couldn't read every one, but they were crossing our screens all day long. So this approach was especially relevant to a tool like Twitter. We had the benefit of being able to watch how people used it. It taught us open-mindedness.

139

If this book were limited to 140 pages,
it would end here.

I had thought that what I was doing was building a company that was true to my ideals, but what actually happened along the way is that I built a brand. The Twitter brand became recognizable and strong. We attracted so much press and intellectual brain space that we were prematurely lumped in with Facebook—in truth, we were a tiny fraction of its size.

Our first holiday party, in December of 2008, took place in the wine room of Millennium, a vegan restaurant in San Francisco where we'd also held the Odeo holiday parties. Around a dozen employees, we were small enough to fit into the back room. I recently found the old slide show from that party. We were still keeping mum about how many users we had. The truth was that we were up to 685,000 registered people, from 45,000 at SXSW. Not bad for a project that was just over a year old. But the media buzz was that we had ten million users. Whenever people asked me how many we had, I always said, "The number of users doesn't matter. All that matters is that people are finding the service interesting and useful." Sticking to our own rules was paying off. The brand was huge before the service was huge.

Two years later the day would come when we hit, then surpassed, 100 million users. In 2010, at the first and only Chirp Conference, a professional gathering for the Twitter development community, I got up onstage and said the same thing I'd always said: "The number of users doesn't matter. All that matters is that people are finding the service interesting and useful." But this time, as I said it, I clicked the Next button to show a new slide I'd just added to my talk. It read, "140 million." Even humility has a time and place.

141

12

YOU CAN HANDLE THE TRUTH

In March of 2009, I celebrated my thirty-fifth birthday. I tweeted,

> Today's my birthday. I'm in my thirties!

A snarky gossip website caught on to the mislead and tried to make something of it, but I had merely been amusing myself with one of my mentor Steve Snider's old games: offering two truths that amount to a lie. Once, I went out to dinner to Golden Era, a Chinese restaurant in Brookline, with him and his family, and someone said to him, "Oh, is this your son?" Steve responded, "Marlene and I were married in 1973, and Biz was born a year later." Two true but unrelated statements that made his answer to the question seem like a yes.

When I first worked as a freelance designer, I made my company a website. To liven up the home page, I scanned in a beautiful picture from the Pottery Barn catalogue, showing a gorgeous office overlooking a garden. One day, I went to a meeting at a school. It was for a good gig, one I really wanted, designing a whole series of books. The women I met with said, "We really like your office." I was actually working out of the dank basement of my mom's house then, so at first I had no idea what she was talking about. Then it dawned on me. She thought that Pottery Barn picture was my office.

I didn't lie. Not exactly. I just said, "Oh, yeah. It's a dream office."

When Livia and I lived briefly in LA, we had two cats even though we weren't allowed to have pets in our apartment. Livia was always worried that the landlady would check in and see the cats. I said, "Here's what you do. If the landlady comes by and says, 'I see that you have cats,' what you say is 'We have friends who are out of town. We're taking care of these cats.'" Both of those sentences were true. We had lots of out-of-town friends back in Boston. And we were absolutely taking care of those cats.

I guess my point is that even at thirty-five, I was still willing to stretch the truth a little bit to give the impression I wanted to give. In other words, I was a bit of a clown. But things were getting more serious.

13

THE NO-HOMEWORK POLICY

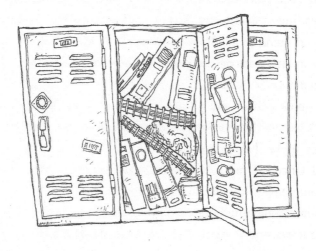

We were in the game, and—from how we responded to our users to how we interacted with governments to how much we were worth—we got to make our own rules.

My earliest experience making my own rules came when I entered high school. In the first weeks of my freshman year, I tried to do everything right. I did exactly what I was told to do—and this included my homework. After lacrosse practice and my after-school job as a box boy at a local supermarket, I got home around 8:00 p.m. At this point, I was expected to eat dinner, do homework, and go to sleep so I could wake up and do it all over again.

The first weeks of my freshman year, I forged ahead with this plan. There was a certain amount of reading for history class, problems to be solved for math, and similar nightly assignments from English, political science, chemistry, biology, and more. The workload added up, and I'm not particularly fast at reading or doing any of that kind of work, for that matter. In fact, I tend to take longer than most people to absorb information and work on problems. But that first week, I was determined to get it all done. If everyone else was doing it, so would I.

I quickly discovered that trying to complete all the homework assigned to me meant staying up almost all night long every night. I couldn't quit lacrosse—I'd created the team! And I needed my job in order to contribute to the family income. My mother's jobs, when she could get them, were not enough to pay the bills. She'd sold the house she grew up in for a lesser house, banking the profit so we had money to live on. That had lasted a while, and then she'd had to do it again. We'd moved a bunch of times. By high school, the house we lived in had an actual dirt floor downstairs and walls without plaster. Now I could honestly say that we were "dirt poor." My mom and I did our best to improve the house on the weekends, but we always needed more money.

This whole homework thing clearly wasn't going to work. I decided to take matters into my own hands and implement a "No-Homework Policy." My plan was simple. I would work as hard as possible to pay attention and be completely focused in each class, but I would not bring my books home, and I would not do any of the homework assigned to me. If the homework was intended to reinforce what was taught in class, I would be fine—because I would make sure to absorb it all during the school day. Once I landed on this solution, a sense of relief washed over me. All that was left was the small matter of communicating my new policy to my teachers.

The next day, one by one, I walked each of my teachers through my plan. The conversation went pretty much the same with all of them: First, I said hello and reintroduced myself. Then I explained that I'd been attempting to do all my home-work for the past two weeks. (I may also have hinted that per-haps the teachers might communicate with one another more about how much work they were assigning to students.) I told them that doing the work took me until approximately 4:00 a.m. Regrettably, I was unable to sustain this. Then I intro-duced my No-Homework Policy.

Some of the teachers laughed, but ultimately all of them told me in their own ways that if I really wanted to go ahead with this, I could, but it would affect my overall grade. I was willing to live with that.

From that point on, I didn't do homework. I paid attention in class and strived to absorb the material. Ultimately, per-haps because I had been so up front and clear in my commu-nication of the policy, my teachers did not end up penalizing me. In other words, my No-Homework Policy didn't have an impact on my overall grades. It was, for all intents and pur-poses, a rousing success.

I distinctly remember the reaction one of my friends in

high school had to this policy. Matt was a great student, but it didn't seem to come easy for him. Though he worked very hard, he had quite a bit of anxiety about taking tests and quizzes, and about his grades in general. At the end of one day in the middle of our freshman year, we were both at our lockers. Matt was loading his backpack up with books. I was dumping all my books from my backpack into my locker, not to be seen again until school the next day.

As I closed my locker and it was apparent to Matt that I had no books, not to mention a backpack, Matt asked me how I was going to do my homework.

"Oh," I said. "I have a No-Homework Policy."

Matt looked incredulous. He laughed nervously. "You're joking."

"Matt," I said, having a little fun with him. "This is America. We can do whatever we want. Freedom. I have a No-Homework Policy and it's great."

I shut my locker with unusual emphasis and headed to lacrosse practice, unencumbered.

I wasn't against rules per se; I just liked to look at the big picture. Staying up until four in the morning wasn't realistic. Something had to give.

The point of this story isn't "cocky kid blows off homework and gets away with it," though on the surface that's exactly what happened. Homework is generally regarded as useful, and far be it from me to mount a one-man campaign against it. (Not right now, anyway. Talk to me when my kid is twelve.) But I had an idea for a different way to do things, one that worked better for me. There was no harm in proposing this to the school administration. There was no danger in trying. The point of school, after all, isn't to do homework. The point of school is to learn. When I realized this, I stopped caring about grades. As high school progressed, I focused on learning what inspired me, so I might get an A+ in genetics and a C in something easy. I was by no means a model student, but I deliberately, consciously chose my path. It was a mistake to assume that teachers—or anyone else, for that matter—automatically knew what was best for me. If I could better accomplish the mutually agreed-upon goal through my own approach, wasn't it worth a shot?

If anything, opportunities like this are easier to recognize and implement in the workplace. Do you work best in a dimly lit room? Do you perform better with an afternoon nap? Would you like to work on a side project that is more interesting to you? Is there a different way to think about your business? Rules are there to help us—to create a culture, to streamline productivity, and to promote success. But we're not computers that need to be programmed. We're all a bunch of oddballs. Just because someone has authority doesn't mean they know better. If you approach your bosses or colleagues with respect, and your goals are in alignment, there's often room for a little customization and flexibility. And on the other side, those in positions of power shouldn't force people to adhere to a plan for the sake of protocol. The solution, always, is to listen carefully—to your own needs and to those of the people around you.

My irreverence came into play again when I went to my first high school dance. Ordinarily I didn't rise to the social challenge of high school functions—especially not dances. The anxiety and embarrassment quotients were just too high. Plus, my friends and I were nerds, so what free time we had we preferred to devote to reading comic books or playing video games.

However, near the end of my senior year, as my friend Jay and I sat in his attic reading *Batman* comics, it occurred to me that the absolutely last dance we'd ever get the opportunity to attend as high school kids was scheduled for that very night. I put down my comic book.

"Jay, we can't miss the dance tonight."

He looked up with some surprise. After all, we always missed the dances. "Why not?" he said.

"It's a rite of passage. This is our last chance." All of a sudden, I was completely impassioned. I made an impromptu speech about how important this moment was and how we couldn't let it pass us by or we would regret it for the rest of our lives. Twenty years from now, when we were old men of thirty-eight, we would sit in rocking chairs on a front porch somewhere, shaking our heads with disappointment at the tragic choices of our younger selves. (But, I paused to muse, we'd definitely have cars and be allowed to drive them by then. Cool.) Seriously, though, we had to go to the dance.

Jay sighed and put down his comic book. He could see that I wasn't going to let this go.

Even now that Jay was somewhat persuaded, this eleventh-hour decision was going to be tricky to execute. It was already 8:40, and the doors to the dance closed in twenty minutes.

149

There was a strict rule that nobody could be admitted after 9:00 p.m. Neither of us had a driver's license or a car. We'd have to get on our bicycles and ride like hell to get there in time.

We pedaled furiously down the streets of Wellesley, but as we approached the school cafeteria, ready to pay our six-dollar entry fee, we saw that the doors were closed. Standing in front of them, like a prison guard, was the vice principal. We were two minutes late, max.

Panting, I managed to say, "We're here for the dance."

"You're too late. The doors are closed," the vice principal said drily.

"Okay, I understand," I said.

Jay gave me a curious look. He knew me well enough to wonder why, after my passionate declamation, I wasn't smooth-talking my way in. Normally I would have tried, but I could see from the vice principal's demeanor that tonight that approach wouldn't fly.

I turned around and said, "C'mon Jay, let's do something else."

Jay suspected something was up, and he was right. There was no way I'd give up that easily. We had to attend this dance. My resolve was as strong as it had been for the past twenty-two minutes. As we walked away from the doors, and the vice principal, I muttered to Jay, "We're still getting in."

We crept around to the other side of the cafeteria, where there were giant tilt-in windows. Surely they would be open, to ventilate a cafeteria full of sweaty teenagers. Climbing in would be a piece of cake.

Sure enough, the windows were open. We slipped in. A few kids noticed, but what did they care?

"We're in, Jay. This is it. Our last-ever high school dance. Let's make it count!"

In our high-speed plot session, Jay and I had decided that we'd put aside all insecurities, assume false bravado (an early manifestation of Biz Stone, Genius), and ask the girls we'd always had crushes on to dance with us. We turned around to do just that—and there he was. Vice Principal Buzzkill. His jaw dropped when he saw us. Busted. He ordered us to follow him upstairs to his office.

We trudged up the stairs, first the vice principal, then me, with Jay bringing up the rear. When we got to the top and started down the hall toward his office, I was hit by a sudden impulse. By George, I was going to stick to my plan, come hell or high water. While the vice principal walked briskly forward, I spun around and started back down the stairs.

As I whisked by, I whispered to Jay, "We're still doing this."

Jay hesitated for a moment, frozen, eyes wide. At that moment, the vice principal must have turned back. He yelled something down the stairs in the direction of the cloud of dust I'd left behind. Jay bolted after me. The chase was on!

I bounded quickly to the bottom of the stairs, where I bumped into one of my best friends, Marc Ginsburg. Marc and I had grown up together. As a kid, I had practically lived at his house. His dad was a successful dentist, so he'd bought the family an Apple IIe that we used constantly. Marc was taller than me, but he had similar hair and features. When

I spotted him, I said, "Don't ask me why, but switch T-shirts with me right now."

Marc, a true friend, complied instantly and without question. Soon he was wearing my black T-shirt, and I was wearing his yellow T-shirt. I scampered out of sight, then turned around from a safe distance to watch as the vice principal grabbed Marc by the shoulder, whipped him around, then apologized when he realized he had the wrong kid.

During that confrontation, Jay slipped into the safety of the crowd, where we reconvened.

We'd made it.

We got right down to business. That evening, I managed to dance with all three of the girls I had crushes on but had been too intimidated to talk to the whole time I attended high school. I even got a little kiss from each one. Jay had a similar experience, and I felt vindicated. High school was ending, and for the first time in my life I didn't know what was next. The too-blank canvas of my future would underwhelm me, but at least I was making the most of tonight. The dance had turned out to be everything we wanted. Whatever punishment we got would be worth it.

On Monday, it was time to face the music. Jay and I were summoned to the principal's office. He told us that we would be placed under "in-house" suspension. That meant that we would sit in separate rooms all day; we wouldn't attend classes; and of course this would go on our "permanent record." (Was there really such a thing? And if there was, I couldn't help but wonder in what terms it chronicled my No-Homework Policy.) We also had to write an essay about what we had done wrong, after which we would each pay a mandatory visit to the school psychologist.

This all sounded perfectly reasonable to me. In fact, it was a much lighter sentence than I had anticipated. I was especially pleased by the essay component. I loved writing essays. Indeed, when I sat down in the empty detention hall to write it, I realized in a flash that this essay was the perfect forum for me to explain why, in this case, our breaking the rules had been fully warranted and totally worth it. Rules are meant to serve a purpose, but the "9:00 p.m. doors closed" policy was pointless as far as Jay and I were concerned. To us it was an abuse of power. We weren't troublemakers. Our tardiness had had no impact on anyone else. The dance was important to us, and in the face of the vice principal's inflexibility, we had seen no choice but to defy him and risk the consequences. Now we were willingly serving our punishment. For good measure, I threw in some civil disobedience references from my political science class. I crossed my fingers that Jay was doing the same thing.

Later that day, it came time for me to visit with the school psychologist. I knocked on her door. She told me to come in and take a seat. I sat down. There was a beat of silence. Then she launched into how convincing my essay was, and how she couldn't help but agree with the decisions I'd made.

When I met up with Jay at the end of the day, I was delighted to learn that he had taken the same approach in his essay. Breaking the rules wasn't the end of the world. We had stood our ground against the administration, and we had won. No harm, no foul. This was a small disobedience but a significant moment for a teenager. I knew the difference between right and wrong. But now I saw that I could trust my own moral code. The rule makers were fallible, just like me, and I had every right to challenge them. If I was willing to face the consequences, I could play by my own rules.

Trust your instincts, know what you want, and believe in your ability to achieve it. Rules and conventions are important for schools, businesses, and society in general, but you should never follow them blindly. And it always helps to have a like-minded partner in crime.

14

THE NEW RULES

Sixteen years later, I was still the same kid who didn't think he had to listen to the vice principal. Following my instincts now didn't just mean blowing off my homework, crashing high school dances, and setting the value of our company by making a joke while wearing a bad shirt and riding shotgun in a Porsche. It meant growing a company I could believe in. As I said, I was truly passionate about the product, but I was also passionate about who we were as a company—what our culture was and how we could sustain it as we grew. It wasn't a matter of breaking the rules; it was about creating our own rules. I made Twitter into a company that was true to my beliefs.

———

The unofficial internal motto at Google is Don't Be Evil. The idea is that the company should do good in the world even if it means forgoing short-term gains. It's not the worst motto—I mean, there's always Be Evil—but there's wiggle room in Don't Be Evil. The motto sounds morally aboveboard. It implies, "We have the power to be evil; let's not use it." But aphorisms phrased in the negative are weak. Nike's motto is Just Do It— not Don't Just Sit There. With its motto, it appears that Google is measuring its actions on a scale of evilness rather than on a scale of goodness. To that I say, congratulations. You haven't been evil. Now let's see how good you can be.

Another thing I noticed when I worked at Google was that we had a different approach to the intersection of people and technology. Google is made up of geniuses. They are awesome at developing technology. They're making self-driving cars. Seriously, it's a car driving around all by itself. No driver. Quite a feat, but also representative of Google's world, where technology can solve any problem. On my breaks while working there, walking around the campus, I liked to peek into rooms. Once, I peeked into a room and saw a guy with no shoes on. He was sitting in the middle of the floor surrounded by disassembled DVRs and TVs.

I said, "What are you doing?"

He said, "I'm recording everything being broadcast on every channel in the world."

"Okay," I said, "Keep up the good work," and backed slowly out of the room.

Another time, I stumbled across a vast roomful of people operating what looked like foot-pedal sewing machines. Each machine emitted a sequence of florescent flashes and whirs. The place resembled a high-tech sweatshop. I looked closer. In between the flashes of light, these "tailors" were turning the pages of books, which were being scanned by the lights. When I asked the workers what they were up to, they told me they were scanning every book ever published. Again, I backed slowly out of the room. I backed out of a lot of rooms at Google.

Google has a strong focus on technology, and it serves them well. My experience there was that they ordered technology first and people second.

I believe the opposite. It isn't all about how many servers you have or how sophisticated your software is. Those things matter. But what really makes a technology meaningful—to its users and its employees—is how people come to use it to effect change in the world.

I don't mean to throw Google under the bus. Obviously they're brilliant. It's just that my priorities are flipped. People come before technology.

As Twitter expanded rapidly, I decided that the best way to indoctrinate new employees to our culture was to give them a set of assumptions I wanted them to carry with them as they went about their work.

We make assumptions all day long about the world we live in and the people who inhabit it. The guy who cut you off on the highway entrance ramp is an asshole. The colleague who didn't deliver what she promised is incompetent. If I spent all week working on a problem, my proposal is better than that of the person who waltzed in late to the meeting and threw out an off-the-cuff alternative. What matters most, at any company except a nonprofit, is the bottom line.

If we probe what's behind our assumptions, what we find isn't knowledge or wisdom. It's fear. We're afraid that other people's ideas will make us look *less than*. We're afraid that if we make a change, a product won't come in on time. We're afraid that the guy who cut us off is going to hit our car. We're afraid if we don't maximize our profit, the company will fail. Some of these fears are reasonable. Who wants to be in a car accident? But fear in the absence of knowledge breeds irrationality. Think about the old, universal belief that thunder meant the gods must be angry. This assumption could get people only so far. Maybe they'd avoid being struck by lightning. But were they about to discover how to channel electricity? Not so much.

When I was little, I was afraid of the dark. I signed on to the classic childhood fear that there were monsters under my bed. For a while I had an agreement with the monsters. *I totally believe in you*, I told them telepathically. *No need to come out and prove it to me. I'm on board.* This seemed to keep them at bay, but even I could see it was only a temporary fix.

158

After some months of dread, I had an idea. I decided to put an end to my suffering. My plan was simple. I would go into my room and leave the light off, thereby exposing myself to all the terrors the dark might hold. If there were monsters, this was their big chance to attack me. My thought was that if they attacked me—well, that would be pretty bad. On the other hand, I mused, if monsters attacked me, then that would mean that monsters actually existed—which would be awesome. Initially scary, sure, but then, imagine! The thrill of discovering the existence of a whole supernatural world out there was right at my fingertips. All I had to do was endure a monster attack of unpredictable proportions, and this knowledge would be mine—possibly only for a fraction of a second, before I was torn to shreds and used to make little boy stew, but still. That night, I walked into my room without flicking on the light switch. I stood in the dark, waiting. Nothing. No monsters. No attack. No world-altering discovery of inhuman life forms. And also, from then on, no fear of the dark.

We should always seek knowledge, even in the face of fear. And so I gave the Twitter employees a set of assumptions that I hoped would replace their fears, reminding them to keep their minds open, pursue knowledge, and see the bigger picture.

When new employees joined Twitter, Evan and I met with them. We took the time to tell the story of how the company got started, and we shared and discussed the following six assumptions.

Assumptions for Twitter Employees

1. We don't always know what's going to happen.
2. There are more smart people out there than in here.
3. We will win if we do the right thing for our users.
4. The only deal worth doing is a win-win deal.
5. Our coworkers are smart and they have good intentions.
6. We can build a business, change the world, *and* have fun.

WE DON'T ALWAYS KNOW WHAT'S GOING TO HAPPEN.

If we think we know what will come next, we'll fail. Instead, we need to leave the door open for unknown developments and surprises. Some of Twitter's most popular features—hashtags, @ replies, retweets—were by and large created by users. We didn't know they were going to emerge. By being open to the unknown, by not forcing our will or vision just because it was ours, by watching what people were doing and looking for patterns, we were able to build a service whose function matched the way people wanted to use it.

The core element of this assumption is humility. Just because you work for a successful business doesn't mean you know everything. As individuals and as companies, we see our fortunes rise and fall. Neither success nor wealth makes you omniscient. The ability to listen, watch, and draw lessons from obvious and unlikely places breeds originality and growth.

THERE ARE MORE SMART PEOPLE OUT THERE THAN IN HERE.

This assumption also speaks to a core humility—don't think you're such a genius (even if your business card claims you are). But it also considers the sheer fact that, at the time we came up with these assumptions, there were forty-five people in the offices of Twitter and six billion people outside its walls. It was an absolute truth that there were more smart people outside than inside.

What this implied was that we shouldn't look only internally for answers to challenges. I instructed our employees to look elsewhere. Ask people. Look around. Research. Keep a level head. Don't think you're so great. Don't assume that we're the only people who can solve our problems. Should we build a data center, or has someone already built a better one?

There are corollaries to this belief. Your first idea isn't always the best. *Your* idea isn't always the best. Our group's ideas aren't always the best. It's easy to agree with this notion in concept, but it's much harder to swallow your pride when you have to let go of an idea you've championed. I wanted our company to acknowledge and appreciate those sacrifices as much as we applauded the great ideas.

WE WILL WIN IF WE DO THE RIGHT THING FOR OUR USERS.

I don't love the word *users*, because it sounds so software-y, but the Twitter staff was pretty software-y, so I was speaking their language. I wanted them always to keep in mind what would make the service better for the folks who used it. It was the positive spin on Don't Be Evil. Every time we made a decision about what to add, change, or take away from the product, the big, simple question was: Does it make the experience better for people?

After I left (which I will get to later), Twitter acquired Vine, a mobile video-sharing service. I thought it was a great acquisition. If the question is: Will this make the service better for people? The answer is obviously yes—sharing videos through Twitter makes it more fun, more engaging, and easier for people to express themselves.

Often, when product managers are hashing out whether a product should do a certain thing, if they can't come to a decision, they make that thing a setting that users can turn on or off. But this is wishy-washy. We know—all developers know—that more than 99 percent of people just leave the settings on the default. How often do you go into your TV settings to increase the contrast? Making a feature optional is like throwing it into the junk drawer. You're keeping it, but it's essentially useless and lost. Instead, it's our responsibility to decide what makes the most sense. If we're going to build it, let's use it.

The place where companies most frequently lose sight of what's best for their customers is when it comes to monetization. Should we make ads 50 percent bigger so we can make more money? It makes the page ugly and hard to read. Is that good for users? *No.* Should we split our company into two separate buildings because we can't afford one building? It leads to confusion and poor decisions on the product end. Is that good for our users? *No.* Should we deceive the user into clicking on an ad? *Obviously not.* Should we trick our users into clicking on anything? *Hell no!* These can be tough choices, especially if you really need the money. But there's got to be another way. Creativity is a renewable resource. Don't sell out your product. Keep thinking. Consider whether the average person is going to benefit. Measure every decision against that requirement.

Our failure surrounding the release of our platform for developers in 2007 is a perfect example of this. If we'd kept the user experience foremost from the start, we would have saved ourselves, users, and developers a lot of trouble.

However, when we launched sponsored Tweets, we did it right. Our ads were monitored by an algorithm that used starring, retweets, and clickthroughs to measure how interested people were in a given ad. If an ad wasn't getting a positive response, it could be pulled. This meant we could give our users ads they liked. Ads were good for our users, because if Twitter made money, then Twitter would continue to exist.

THE ONLY DEAL WORTH DOING IS A WIN-WIN DEAL.

There's no such thing as a good deal in which one party gets the short end of the stick. Deals are like relationships. We want deals that are going to last. I'm not just talking about acquiring another company. I'm talking about partnering with another company, or divvying up tasks within your group, or getting married. Think of the toll that derivatives took on this country in the mortgage crisis. Derivatives are a zero-sum game—when one party wins, the other loses. There's no net benefit. It's win-lose. This is of course oversimplifying, but generally markets rely on gains and losses. However, in a business deal, if the terms aren't mutually beneficial, a short-term win will turn into a long-term loss. You lose that company's faith in you and its willingness to do another deal. You lose your colleagues' willingness to stay late and help you out on a deadline. To some extent, in every deal your reputation and your business are at stake. Think of it like scuba diving. There has to be equal pressure inside and outside your body, or your lungs and eardrums will start exploding. Full disclosure: I've never scuba dived—but trust me on this, imbalance is bad.

Kevin Thau, a colleague at my current company, Jelly, used to run all things mobile for Twitter. While there, he did all the deals with the carriers. He recently got a message from someone who runs a major mobile carrier in the United Kingdom. It said, "I don't know what Jelly is, but if you want us to preinstall it on our new phones, call me." Nobody gets that kind of thing unless they have a history of doing fantastic deals together.

Another example of this would come later, when I left Twitter and started Jelly. Two of the people who helped me develop the idea left their company to join me. One of them happened to be on his company's list of engineers they couldn't lose at any cost. When the engineer told them he was leaving, they offered him the moon regarding stock and salary. They told him he could work on any project and have any team. Then one of the most important executives from Twitter joined me. I didn't set out to poach anyone—it happened by accident— but when this happened, Dick Costolo, Twitter's CEO (and my friend) had a professional obligation to meet me for a drink and chew me out.

When he was done busting my chops, I said, "Can I offer you a little advice?"

He said, "Oh, geez. What?"

I said, "If you have a list of people that you don't want to lose at any cost, don't wait until they quit to offer them more money and more stock options." He agreed. Then we ordered another round and made up.

OUR COWORKERS ARE SMART AND THEY HAVE GOOD INTENTIONS.

This is the fifth assumption I presented to our employees at orientation. I made up an example: Imagine there's a guy named Scott in Marketing who lays out a plan for a product you're developing. He says it will take three months to execute. Three months later, the product is ready to launch, and Scott comes forward with a different, scaled-back plan. It's not as good as the one he presented to you. Instead of assuming that Scott is lazy or a stupid jackass, why not go up to him and introduce yourself? *Hi, I'm Biz. How can I help?*

You don't know how it all unfolded. There were certain turns in the road, decisions that had to be made. You went through the same process with the product you developed. It was supposed to have features w, x, and y, but now it has x and z. You had to pare it down, but you're still proud of it. You don't want Scott to think you're an idiot, either. In big, unwieldy companies, everyone starts looking like an idiot at some point.

The unknown is scary. That's why a caveman would rather not walk into a pitch-black cave. Who knows what might lie ahead? He opts to throw his spear in first, or to bolt. In a business scenario, this fear manifests itself in the assumption that your colleague is doing it wrong. But instead of throwing a spear, you assume he's the enemy. Communication is equivalent to flicking on the anachronistic lights in that pitch-black cave. This is especially true when you're the CEO. If investors and board members don't hear from you, they get worried that you're doing a bad job. And they're not going to come down to the offices to design a new product. The only power they have at their disposal is to fire the person in charge.

As Twitter grew, we had to go on faith, assuming that our coworkers, who had all gone through a careful hiring process, were competent and driven. Maybe Scott *is* a jackass—hey, it happens—but that shouldn't be the assumption. Imagine if everyone operated with a level of shared confidence. Maybe we would live in an environment of overinflated optimism, but people shine when you give them the benefit of the doubt.

WE CAN BUILD A BUSINESS, CHANGE THE WORLD, *AND* HAVE FUN.

It may sound like a lofty goal, but I want to redefine capitalism. What better place to start than in my own company? Traditionally, companies are driven by financial success. But I want the new definition to include making a positive impact on the world—*and* loving your work. I want to set a higher bar for success. If any one of these three tenets is missing, then you shouldn't be considered successful by your own terms or those of society. I told every incoming employee, "Here's a new bar. Let's reach for it."

Evan and I were now running an incredibly successful company. We could have sent the new employees who joined Twitter to Human Resources and called it a day. Or we could have said, "Welcome to the amazing world of Twitter. We're awesome. Good luck." We had a different approach. The company culture was introduced to our newest employees as one in which we listened to one another and the people using our system. New employees saw that we cared about the approach they took not just to their work, but to one another. They realized that we weren't all about the bottom line. Not only did our new employees have an introduction to what the company was about, but they also learned something about their leaders. We were levelheaded. We had theories about not being arrogant and selfish. We weren't jerks. These things matter. The whole of this orientation was greater than the sum of its parts.

15

TWENTY-FIVE DOLLARS GOES A LONG WAY

When I was little I always dreamed that I could fly. Later, that sensation evolved into believing I could one day do something extraordinary, but I had no idea what that might be, and I never seemed to be on the right path. Then, in early 2009, I was invited to be a guest representing Twitter on *The Colbert Report*. If there was any reliable way of tracking when I'd made it, this was it. The producers of a TV show that I really liked wanted me to come on the show and talk about what I was doing. As far as I was concerned, that invitation meant I'd accomplished something extraordinary. Why else would Stephen Colbert want to talk to me? It was a big moment. Twitter had officially made it over the startup hurdle, and I was flying. Now that Twitter was huge, I wanted to make sure we used our powers for good. That instinct felt like it'd always been with me, but there are a few early moments that I know contributed to my growing sense of how I wanted to be in the world.

First, in high school, I remember a girl asking me if I liked a painting she'd made. I said, "No, I don't like it." She was crushed. What kind of stupid answer was that? I'd upset her. We all have moments like this in our childhoods—moments that nobody else involved would remember, but when a light bulb goes off and your perspective is forever shifted. That moment, when I hurt my amateur artist classmate's feelings, I matured into someone with empathy. I didn't want to walk around upsetting people. I wanted to be a good guy.

Not long after that exchange, I watched an old Jimmy Stewart movie called *Harvey*. In it, Jimmy Stewart befriends a six-foot-tall invisible rabbit. People think he's gone mad, but in the face of their accusations and ridicule, he reveals himself to be persistently good-natured and kind. Again I asked myself, *Am I nice to everyone? Shouldn't I be?* I wasn't a monster before, but *Harvey* inspired me to be actively nice. To be a good guy to everyone. It seemed like a really fine idea, and as I started putting it into practice, I found that I liked it. This may sound a little sociopathic—I *chose* to be nice because it *worked* for me—

but don't we all evolve based on how we interact with the world? It was very basic. I tried out kindness, and it felt right.

Then there was my father. On Sundays, Dad had visiting privileges with me and my sister, Mandy. He'd pick us up at noon, take us to Papa Gino's for lunch, then to mini-golf or a movie. It was an innocuous enough schedule, but that was the toughest day of my week. My father had been out of the picture since I was four, so I'd never had a chance to form a real connection with him. Sundays, therefore, were an anxious time. When I was sixteen, it finally occurred to me that I could refuse to go. If I could not do homework, then I could also not see my father. From then on I elected to play Nintendo with my friend Mark instead. But if I learned anything from those painful Sundays, it was this: my dad wasn't an ideal parent, but I didn't waste time resenting him or blaming myself. I can't say I thought it through; I just turned my attention in a different direction. Given that the world was an imperfect place, I resolved to try to make it as nice as I could. I wanted to find the good—not just to spin things in a positive way (though I'm prone to that, too), but to do my part to make the world a better place.

The Colbert Report wasn't just a sign that I'd made it. The experience also managed to open my eyes to the ripple effect of altruism through a seemingly small gesture: a twenty-five-dollar gift card.

Livy and I really love *The Colbert Report*, and we had a couple of friends who worked at the wild animal hospital with Livy who were also huge fans. We asked and got permission for them to come with us to New York and join us at the taping of the show.

Before I went on the air, Livy and I waited with our friends in the green room. A half hour or so before showtime, Colbert stopped by. He welcomed us warmly and explained to me, "On my show I play a character, and that character is, for lack of a better word, a jackass."

I said, "I know! We love the show!"

He said, "Plenty of people don't know, and sometimes they get upset."

I introduced Livy and her friends, and told Colbert about the wild animal ER where they worked.

Colbert asked about their work and talked to them about some of his wildlife activism: a leatherback sea turtle he'd endorsed, to bring attention to sea turtle endangerment, and an eagle he'd helped rehabilitate. I was impressed. Instead of projecting *I'm Stephen Colbert and I have my own TV show*, he showed an interest in what our friends did and took the time to have a genuine conversation about it.

After the show, Livy and I were given a gift basket. Its contents were probably similar to what lots of TV shows hand out: a *Colbert* hat, a T-shirt, a bottle of water. That sort of thing. But there was one small item in the basket that would have a huge effect on me. It was a twenty-five-dollar gift card to DonorsChoose.org.

DonorsChoose.org is a uniquely structured online charity that benefits schools. Public school teachers across America post requests on the site for materials they need for their classrooms. You can contribute to a project that interests you, or a school in your neighborhood, or the classroom of a teacher who sounds amazing or in great need. The money you give is put toward the exact materials the teacher has requested and priced.

Livia and I gave our friends the hat and the T-shirt, but we took the DonorsChoose.org card home with us. Back in Berkeley, we went on the website together. We found a second-grade class that needed copies of *Charlotte's Web*, and we donated the number the teacher said she needed. It was so cool.

Livia and I were happy to help, but the best part came a few weeks later, when we got mind-blowingly cute thank-you notes from every kid in the class.

———

Empathy is the ability to understand and share the feelings of others. Most of us are born with this gift, but not all of us have learned how to access it readily or how to use it in productive and meaningful ways. Here was a child thanking me in her own tentative words and determined hand. What better way to trigger genuine empathy than through a charity that creates a direct connection between the givers and the recipients?

When I was a kid and I walked past a bell-ringing Salvation Army Santa on my way into the supermarket, I'd always drop some loose change into his bucket. But Santa's pail was a black hole. I never had the slightest idea where my quarters went, or whether they actually made a difference. And certainly nobody was ever going to come up to me and say, "Hey, thanks for the quarter. That turned out to be the last quarter we needed. World hunger: solved." There was no expectation of thanks, success, or even a sense of the results of the effort.

But that was okay. I wasn't looking for feedback or thank-yous. I just saw giving to others as part of being a person.

With DonorsChoose.org, that feeling of blindly donating disappeared. My gift had immediate results, the recipients shared their gratitude, and this made me want to give more. It was a brilliant feedback loop. Empathy requires more imagination than when you throw a coin into a pot. When you get a heartfelt letter from a kid who has experienced the friendship of Charlotte and Wilbur for the first time—well, that child springs to life. You see the need, and the path to filling it. Livy and I started regularly donating to DonorsChoose.org. We didn't have much money yet—we were only giving fifty dollars at a time—but we were really into it. On any given night, you can spend your evening watching a sitcom or two, or you and your spouse can help some kids. Which feels better?

From DonorsChoose.org, I discovered the aforementioned powerful feedback loop of altruism, but there was another, perhaps even bigger lesson, and it was this: if Stephen Colbert hadn't given me that twenty-five-dollar gift card, I wouldn't have helped those children. It didn't change the world, but it helped a few teachers do the projects they wanted to do. And I like to think that each of those kids who read *Charlotte's Web* gained something from the book that will last forever and have a reverberating effect. The kids also had the experience of receiving a gift from a stranger. So now it's not just me that Stephen reached. His gift reached the teacher, those kids, and the people that their positive experience and intellectual growth will touch. And I'm just *one* of the guests on Colbert's show who received a gift card to DonorsChoose.org. If every one of the recipients—or even a fraction of us—had a similar experience, think of the broad reach of that simple gesture!

At the Chirp Conference, we gave DonorsChoose.org gift cards to all attendees—hundreds, if not thousands, of people got twenty-five dollars to give toward a project on the site, and, according to Charles Best, the charity's founder and CEO, an unusually high number of those people continued to support the project.

Stephen's small act of kindness—his donation in the form of that twenty-five-dollar gift card to each guest on his show—had exponential results. I call this the compound interest of altruism.

Many of us know the value of compound interest: If you have a savings account where the interest you earn gets added to your savings every month, then the next month the interest you earn will be a little bit higher. Repeat that month after month, and your wealth grows at a steep incline. For example, imagine that when you turned twenty you put one hundred dollars in a savings account with an annual interest rate of 0.64 percent compounded monthly. If you continued to put a hundred dollars in every month until you were forty years old, then you'd have $25,724. (Meanwhile, credit cards have average annual interest rates of 15 percent! That's over twenty-three times the interest on your savings account. If you run a hundred-dollar credit card debt for twenty years—adding that same hundred dollars every month and never making payments—you'll owe $153,567 when you're forty!)

This phenomenon is not unique to savings accounts or even money. Stephen's gift card inspired me and Livia to give at the level we could afford at the time.

And then another thing happened. Twitter grew, my financial situation changed, and Livia and I started giving a lot more money to DonorsChoose.org. Charles Best asked to meet us. I helped sketch out a redesign of their website and started otherwise advising him. My relationship with the charity grew and became more personal. Eventually I became a major donor, adviser, and active participant in DonorsChoose.org.

All of this from a twenty-five-dollar gift card.

It's hard to give money when you have very little. Believe me, I spent many years in debt and I know intimately how it feels to worry about every single dollar. But people generally go about philanthropy the wrong way. They think you need to wait until you're comfortable—i.e., rich—to give. We all define financial success differently, but I can tell you that for almost anyone at any income level, being rich exists only in the future.

Waiting to give is a mistake. It doesn't have to be about money. If you get involved early—now—the value of your gift is compounded over time. This is true in two ways. First, setting the habit of thinking of others early, before you have much to give, means that intention matures along with you. As your fortune increases, so does your inclination to give. Second, and perhaps more important, your gifts have a ripple effect, just like Stephen Colbert's gift cards. Over the next two decades, the amount of good you will have done will be exponentially greater than if you'd waited until you were forty or fifty years old to write a check.

It's not all about money. You can give time instead of

cash. Or spread the word the way Colbert did. Or give small amounts that you can afford.

The smallest, earliest gifts forever alter your trajectory for doing good. This is what I mean by the compound interest of altruism. Start early to maximize the compound interest in your efforts.

I wasn't out of debt until 2010. Twitter hadn't yet gone public, but with a successful startup, there are eventually opportunities to sell shares privately to investors. It's an opportunity to take real money out of the theoretical money. I still believed in Twitter, and I certainly didn't sell all my shares, but it didn't make sense to have 100 percent of my money invested in one company. Anyone involved in a startup should take the same opportunity.

So I took money off the table. I distinctly remember the day we closed the deal. The guy who was, at the time, my business manager sent me an email saying, "We just got the wire." It was for a whole big pile of money. More money than I had ever dreamed of.

I responded, "Woot. Thanks, Biz."

He wrote back, "Woot? You're set for life and that's your response?"

Then I went downstairs to Livy and joked, "Okay, we're now officially rich white people who live in Marin."

Nothing really changed, except that I felt an overwhelming sense of relief. I'd grown up poor, and I'd spent almost my entire adult life in debt. Livy's parents were freelance artists living from hand to mouth. Neither of us had been on the streets, but we were never financially secure. We had grown somewhat comfortable being uncomfortable. It seemed like only yesterday that Livy and I were pouring coins from a coffee can into a Coinstar machine and Livy was clapping because we hit one hundred dollars.

The best thing I can say about having enough money after being in debt is that money is an immune system. When you're in debt—and you have to pick which bills to pay and which to default on every month, for years—you're always at the edge. Every little expense is bone on bone. Every choice can easily become an argument between you and your spouse.

If you have enough money—you don't have to be rich, but if you have enough to meet your needs, pay your bills, and put a little in savings—the constant anxiety of just getting by disappears. The persistent worry you were carrying fades. The biggest effect money has had on me is that now, every day, I'm grateful for the relief from that anxiety.

The other thing I'll say about money is that having a lot of it amplifies who you are. I have found this to be almost universally true. If you're a nice person, and then you get money, you become a wonderful philanthropist. But if you're an asshole, with lots of money you can afford to be *more* of an asshole: "Why isn't my soda at sixty-eight degrees Fahrenheit?" You choose who you are no matter what, but I have to say that the anxiety of making ends meet gives you a bit of a pass. When you're rich, you have no excuse.

There's another key aspect of altruism that is ignored when we evaluate the option to give: the mistake people make assuming that altruism is a one-way street. We forget the value of helping others. We are all in this world together. When we help others, we also help ourselves.

The simplest everyday example of this is my veganism. Although I'm a vegan because I care how animals are treated, for me being a vegan isn't about giving something up. Health benefits aside, I gain something from knowing that I've made that choice and am sticking to it. Doing good isn't a sacrifice.

Here's another way of thinking about it. Right now a lot of recent college graduates are having trouble getting jobs. You can go on interviews every day and constantly get rejected. You're drained; it takes a toll on your confidence. So how about this? How about instead you go volunteer at a nonprofit? Suddenly you're busy; you're doing something good; and you're networking along the way. Maybe you'll discover that one of the other volunteers has a lead on a job or has a great contact for you. At the very least, you have something to say at your job interview. "I'm volunteering, but I'm looking for full-time work." You feel good about yourself; you're glowing with the knowledge that you're helping others. You exude confidence and productivity. Now when you go to a job interview, all that depth of experience comes through.

Don't think of helping other people as giving something away or taking something from yourself. Think of what you're gaining. It's a paradox, but helping other people is helping yourself.

Livy and I live modestly on purpose. I like simple, small, cheap things. Timex watches, Levis, and my VW Golf. Occasionally, when Livy sees me playing with our toddler, Jake, at the park, or when he and I are playing on the floor together, I'll see tears in Livy's eyes. I know she's crying out of happiness. These are the moments that matter most in life, and it can happen on any floor in any house or in any park in any neighborhood. Our version of buying a Lamborghini and owning a giant house is that we give away a lot of money to help others. Helping others gives us a feeling of success. It makes our lives meaningful. And it can do the same for you, regardless of how much money you have to give.

16

A NEW DEFINITION FOR CAPITALISM

People are good, and if you give them the right tools, they'll use them for the right thing. In the course of developing large-scale communication systems with social elements—starting Xanga; working at Blogger; reading books, magazines and blog posts; thinking at a high level about blogging, self-organizing systems, and stuff like that—one of the patterns I recognized from early on was that these communities tend to be self-policing. Sure, there's some bad behavior. But there is consistently more good than bad. At Twitter, we didn't need an army of people deleting and blocking accounts. This is why large, unregulated, self-organizing systems with a hundred million people using them can function without much disruption. If people weren't nice, I couldn't do my work. It's quite impressive, but if you think about it, of course we humans must be good at cooperating. If we couldn't get along, how would we build buildings and streets and follow traffic laws (most of the time)? If we weren't nice, we wouldn't have civilization.

I read an article in *Yes!* magazine that pointed out that Darwin believed that compassionate communities flourish best and produce the most offspring. So we evolved to be nice. The article also talked about new research that says that on the plains, our ancestors had to learn to share scavenged carcasses. Selfish people were probably cast out. Humans are tribal, and the researcher Michael Tomasello proposes that we've evolved to work collaboratively. You and I, we were born to cooperate. The good in the world isn't just my hallucinogenic optimism. How do you like that? Science!

And if you give us a simple way to help others, we will.

Sure, sounds great. Make the world a better place. Help others. It's easy to say, but as an individual without resources it's hard to take that beyond a worn-out New Year's resolution. But this is the beauty of the flocking at Twitter. As soon as people gather into groups, their energy can be harnessed. They can move as one. They can make things happen.

As soon as I took an interest in the corporate world, I started paying attention to how companies approach social responsibility. Three days after the tragedy of September 11, 2001, I posted on my blog: "Wow, the Amazon Disaster Relief Fund has raised $4.3 million already and it's growing by the minute." I was impressed by the immediacy with which a website had used its reach to rally support. Causes need people to congregate, and as communities, corporations are perfectly positioned to promote and inspire charity.

I've already talked about my new definition for capitalism. I want companies to prioritize not only enjoying financial success (which is normal) and bringing joy to employees and consumers, but also having a positive impact on the world.

Early on, in July 2007, it occurred to us at Twitter that paying to have water bottled and shipped to our office when clean drinking water flowed from the tap was silly, to say the least. In fact, some might go so far as to say it was socially, ecologically, and financially irresponsible. However, folks need to drink water every day. So we devised an official Twitter Inc. water strategy. First, we stopped delivery of bottled water. Next, we bought a water bottle for every employee. Finally, we installed a filter on the tap so the water was tastier. We decided that when guests visited our offices, we would offer them drinking water from our limited stock of Ethos Water. Ethos is a Starbucks subsidiary that raises awareness of the world water crisis and gives a portion of its profit to help children around the world get clean water.

Twitter's water strategy had a ripple effect. Not only did we live by our ethics, but we publicly acknowledged a global problem—1.1 billion people on our planet don't have access to safe, clean drinking water. The result? The nonprofit Charity: Water became the favored charitable organization for Twitter and our users. Soon cities around the world were hosting "Twestivals" to bring together Twitter communities to raise money and awareness for Charity: Water.

Charity: Water was only the beginning. I kept looking for ways Twitter could have a positive impact on society. When we were fussing with iPods for Odeo, Apple released a red iPod as part of an initiative called Product(RED). I took an interest, and found out that the parent company, (RED), raises funds with the goal of eliminating HIV/AIDS in Africa. I learned from the organization what antiretroviral medication can do for people who are HIV positive. The patients can come back from the brink of death and be able to lead healthy lives. The organization offered a stunning opportunity to help a continent that was devastated by the HIV/AIDS epidemic.

With the program Product(RED), many companies agreed to sell a red version of their products and to contribute a portion of the proceeds to (RED). Nike sold red shoelaces; Amex created a red card. I liked Product(RED) and started buying red things from them. Soon after Twitter launched, I registered @red as a Twitter handle, though (RED) had no use for it then. I figured that if Twitter was successful, organizations would register for Twitter accounts, and I fantasized that one day we would be big enough that companies would ask for an account, and I'd get to say, "I saved your handle for you." And indeed, by the end of 2007, when Twitter was getting a lot of attention, (RED) decided they should get involved in social media. They called Twitter and discovered that someone already had the @red account. The message came to me, and I got to call them back and say, "I'm the one who has the at-red account. It's for you."

For World AIDS Day on December 1, 2009, we turned the major elements of our home page red, added a link to (RED)'s Twitter page, offered a red AIDS Day ribbon (a Twibbon, of course) that users could add to their pages, and set up a hashtag, #red, that would turn your Tweet red to highlight mentions of World AIDS Day. It was the first time Twitter had changed its design for a special event.

And it wasn't just a cute graphic near our logo. Websites offer a deal called a takeover, in which the advertiser buys up all the ad space across a site (and is charged massive amounts to do so). It's more than just banner ads; it's sponsorship of the site. This was essentially what Twitter did for (RED), free of charge. We went red for World AIDS Day. Facebook and Google were participating in World AIDS Day, too, but they would never have changed their sites so dramatically for a charity event.

Although it wasn't a grand scheme, our participation helped Twitter. The press coverage lumped us alongside the big players who supported (RED) that day. This is one of the ways in which altruism pays back. The world can't help but see that your intentions are good, and they respond to that.

I didn't have the money when I worked with (RED) to turn Twitter red for a day, but there was an immediate compound effect. Ashton Kutcher tweeted to the four million Twitter followers he had at the time, telling them to

Get involved #red

He wasn't the only celebrity to do so. And (RED) parlayed our efforts into many other things. To this day Chrysi Philalithes, the chief digital officer at (RED), says, "When Twitter went red, you put us on the map. We got in with other social media."

In 2010 (RED), in partnership with HBO, released a film called *The Lazarus Effect*, directed by Lance Bangs and executive-produced by Spike Jonze. In it, you can see the stunning results of antiretrovirals (ARVs). You meet several Zambians undergoing ARV treatment for HIV/AIDS. These stories are hard to hear, but the film is ultimately uplifting. There's an eleven-year-old girl named Bwalya Liteta. She weighs only twenty-four pounds—she's skeletal, pale, weak. Like the other patients with AIDS, she looks like the walking dead. But with ARVs, two little pills that cost forty cents a day, in a few months' time she is transformed into a strong, healthy child who can live a normal life. The film also introduces us to a woman named Constance Mudenda. In 2004 Constance, who had lost three children to AIDS, tested positive for HIV. She was one of the first patients at a new ARV clinic that opened thanks to (RED). When the film was made, Connie was in good health and supervising three clinics, dismantling the stigma that HIV used to have in the community. (In 2013, still under ARV treatment and still mourning the children she lost, she gave birth to a baby girl, Lubona. Her daughter is HIV-negative, showing the future that ARVs offer.) *The Lazarus Effect*, like the letters from the children of DonorsChoose.org, lets people see how their participation saves the lives of real men, women, and children with hopes and dreams.

Consider the compound effect of the work (RED) does. Ill people get better and return to society. Moms become moms again. Dads are dads again. Teachers go back to teaching. People return to work and school. Over time, (RED) has an actual geoeconomic impact. You can see a village come back to life. And then another one. The whole area starts to stabilize. The black hole of charity that I knew as a child is gone. It's not about a quarter in a bucket. This work has measurable results. HIV/AIDS is a grave but solvable problem. We can wipe out AIDS. And it didn't pass my notice that the cost of those pills for one person is forty cents a day. That rounds out to one hundred and forty dollars a year: Twitter's magic number.

You and I can solve problems for real. One day there will be an AIDS-free generation. It's going to be awesome.

———

In 2009, Twitter's user base grew 1,500 percent, and Twitter Inc. grew 500 percent. Some companies are in business only to make a profit. Some organizations exist exclusively to do good. There are also some businesses that earn profit and then make time to do good. Twitter made a tacit promise to the world that it could be a model for doing business in the twenty-first century. I tried to do my part to create a service that made the world better and profited through the effort.

When folks talk about charity, they often reference Maslow's hierarchy of needs. Twentieth-century psychologist Abraham Maslow's theory is that the first needs we seek to fill are the basics: food, water, sleep, etc. Next we look for safety, which includes employment, morality, health, and property. Once we achieve that, we look for love and belonging. Then we strive for confidence and respect. Assuming success up to this point, we hit the top of Maslow's pyramid and discover a more profound need: justification of our very existence. In times of abundance, it's human nature to seek a more purposeful life. This is often best satisfied by practicing selfless concern for the well-being of others.

Companies historically follow a similar path—considering altruism as a last thought in a long list of needs. This approach is flawed. It does not take into account the compound interest of helping others.

In the spring of 2012 I had the privilege of talking with Bill Clinton at the Clinton Global Initiative University, an annual meeting where the next generation of leaders gathers to discuss and propose solutions to global issues. I'd heard Clinton say, "The most effective global citizens will be those who succeed in merging their business and philanthropic missions to build a future of shared prosperity and shared responsibility," and I asked him to elaborate on why he thought this was important. He said that companies grow by bringing more people into the circle of potential customers. But you can grow only so much if billions of people are shut out. He cited three obstacles to growth: abject inequality (half the world lives on less than two dollars a day), political and financial instability, and climate change and resource depletion. He said that companies need to do two things: first, integrate corporate responsibility into their business strategies, and second, support NGOs to take their efforts further. He gave the example of Walmart. When they realized that climate change was real, they cut their packaging across all stores by 5 percent. This had the equivalent impact of taking 211,000 diesel-burning trucks off the road.

I agreed, and added that companies that don't align themselves with a cause are at a competitive disadvantage. It's not just the right thing to do. Industry is either going to destroy the world or save it. It's in our nature as humans to save ourselves. It'll be good business.

Twitter invested early on in altruism, in part because we believed that being a force for good would make us a stronger company. Corporate culture is traditionally hierarchical, with a structure of rules and behaviors like those I pushed back against when I was in high school. We're given a whole pile of homework when a little extra sleep would go a long way. I wanted Twitter, and other companies following its example, to break out of that mold. We could do business with a higher level of ambition and better ways to measure success. We could embrace our employees' innate desire to do good. There is value in selflessness. Companies must understand this pattern and develop products that deliver deeper meaning. It's important that we recognize value before profit. Challenging the very nature of ambition in business is not a well-worn path. Nevertheless, I wanted us to go out of our way to help others, to feel empathy. I wanted our work to be meaningful and rewarding in a variety of ways.

I told our employees, "We can be a force for good, make lots of money, and laugh while we work."

For a company called Room to Read, a charity founded by John Wood, a former Microsoft employee, Twitter launched our own wine label, called Fledgling. We partnered with a winery, and everyone in the company got a chance to help make the wine. We picked and squeezed grapes and produced two kinds of wine: a pinot noir and a chardonnay. We raised money at a wine tasting at the vineyard, and then we sold and auctioned bottles online. All the money we raised went to Room to Read, which buys books for kids in developing nations. If you think about it, it's symbiotic. If you can't read, you can't tweet. The more readers there are in the world, the bigger Twitter's potential reach.

Our promise was to deliver value before profit, and I told this to our employees every chance I got. Together we were building something that had real potential for positive and enduring global impact. Our work affected the lives of others in scenarios ranging from simple socializing and getting work done to disaster relief and political rebellion. The Twitter employees could augment humanity in productive and meaningful ways, but only if we approached our work in a manner consistent with this promise.

Think about it: value before profit. I've already talked about the value of incorporating altruism into your life. But in what other ways can you expand the culture of good? How can you make it consistent across your activities? Maybe you are part of the Twitter community and can use it as a tool for giving or to enact change. Maybe there is another community—your place of worship, your children's school, your town—where a shift in values could inspire alignment with a cause. Independent giving is generous and meaningful, but when we join forces and flock toward a cause, the effect is dazzling.

17

SOMETHING NEW

The startup I'd helped found was growing into a corporation. In 2010, I began examining how far I had come, what I had learned, and what my goals were for the future.

Twitter now had more than one hundred million registered users on the site. We were hiring aggressively and expanding internationally. We were focused on growth and technical stability.

But change was in the wind.

It started in Japan. In the first days of October, I was in Tokyo fostering Twitter's international relations. I had convinced Livia to come with me by promising her that if she waited out my three days of meetings in Tokyo, we could then spend three days doing what most interested her: traveling to Kyoto to see some of its beautiful temples and shrines.

My second day in Tokyo, a Thursday, I was at a digital conference participating in a panel about hackathons. The next day, among other commitments, I was scheduled to do a You-Tube interview with a famous quadriplegic man who was a fan of Twitter. He used Twitter by holding his phone with his shoulder and tweeting with his tongue. On Saturday, Livia and I were to make the promised pilgrimage to Kyoto.

While I was at the panel, I got a call from Jack Dorsey. He and Evan were my closest friends on the board. Jack said, "Biz, the board is firing Evan. It's going to be announced at the staff meeting tomorrow. They're putting Dick [Costolo] in as the interim CEO. You need to get on a plane and be here tomorrow."

This was a total shocker.

Dick Costolo was our COO. We had first hired him in the summer of 2009, though it started out as a joke. Evan was going on paternity leave. Dick was a friend of ours. He had helped found FeedBurner, a web-feed management provider, and went to Google when it bought his company. He did stand-up comedy. We liked him. Ev had texted him on a whim and said, "Hey, want to be interim CEO while I'm on paternity leave?"

Dick texted back, "Ha ha. Seriously?" or something like that.

Ev called me right after. He said, "I was joking around

about Dick taking over from me as CEO, but I actually think we could hire him. He's talking about moving to California, and he's strong where I'm weak. This could be amazing." So we hired Dick as COO in September 2009.

Evan, Jack, and I had started Twitter together. We were a team. I hoped we'd always be a team. I didn't see this coming.

I said, "Okay, Jack, let me see what I can do. Getting home from Japan by tomorrow is going to be a little tricky."

Jack said, "Get a private jet if you have to. We need you here. The company will pay."

Upset, I called Jason Goldman. He, too, had just heard the news. We talked about what, if anything, we could do to make this better for Evan. But the firing was supposed to be announced the very next day. We needed to buy time.

I said, "What if I can't make it back by Friday? Can we make the case that it will look bad for the company if they fire Ev while I'm in Japan?"

Jason thought it was possible that the board would delay the news to wait for me. If I flew back on Saturday, we would at least have the weekend to strategize.

Then I called Jack back. "Please tell the board that I can't find any planes," I told him. "They're all booked. If they have the meeting without me, it's going to look bad. Plus I'm supposed to interview a quadriplegic. Can you see if we can do it on Monday?"

Jack said, "Okay. I'll let everyone know."

Then I had to break the bad news to Livia. Kyoto would

have to wait until the next time we flew halfway around the world. She'd spent three days hanging out in a hotel room only to fly straight back to San Francisco.

———

On Friday I did the interview with the quadriplegic man; then Livia and I flew home. On the plane, I had time to think about what was happening. It wasn't hard to guess the reasons for Ev's firing. I remembered being in a meeting, reviewing our stats, and noticing that on one random Wednesday we had had a banner day. A million new users had signed up, more than twice our daily average of around three hundred thousand. I asked, "What happened on Wednesday?" The answer was that the service was up and running for a contiguous twenty-four hours. It was that simple. If Twitter hadn't been consistently broken, we'd have had a million new users every day. We were holding up our own success. It was our company; if it ran into a wall it would be because we were driving.

Maybe the board thought that by now we should have been technically stable. We should have been growing faster. We should have had monetizing engineers in place. It was taking forever to find a VP of engineering.

Evan was getting dinged for not making progress quickly enough.

———

I arrived home on Saturday and called two meetings for Sunday in the Twitter offices.

First Evan, Jason, and I met. Evan was stressed out yet still incredulous. He kept covering his face, then opening his hands again to say, "What the hell? I don't believe this!" This was the guy who'd given me my big break. For a long time we'd been collaborators, with similarly aligned goals. We'd built this company together. And he was my friend. It was very hard to process what was happening.

It's a rare founder who makes a successful transition to CEO of a huge company. There are arguments on both sides. Some say founders are founders. They're best at starting companies, and CEOs are best at running them. Others argue that it's best to keep the founder as CEO, find out what support he needs, and give that to him.

Our first CEO, Jack, had a background as a programmer. Evan was a programmer/CEO who had sold Blogger before he had a chance to turn it into a business. Neither truly had career CEO experience. It's fine to learn on the job, but as soon as billions are at stake, people get antsy. You can't blame the board for saying, "This company is growing really fast, and there's nobody's in charge who's done this before."

Evan and Jack are both incredibly talented people. If I had to say what both of them lacked, fundamentally, it was that they weren't communicating enough. At least half the job of CEO is communication—because of human nature. People fear what they don't know. If the board wasn't hearing that things were going well, they assumed that things must be going badly.

Dick Costolo had started several companies. He was older, and he was an experienced CEO. Emotions aside, he was a reasonable choice for the position.

But Ev wasn't being demoted. He was being fired. He was

going to be stripped of his security badge and escorted out of the building! This seemed completely unjust to me. It was so extreme. It would look as if Evan had done something terribly inappropriate, when he hadn't. They may have had issues with his leadership, but there was no reason to give his removal this urgency. People would assume the worst.

The three of us sat in the conference room. I said, "I have an idea. What if the board doesn't fire you?"

Evan, understated as always, said, "Yeah, go on."

We all knew that he was out as CEO. When the board of directors votes on a decision like that, it's immutable. As the Borgs of *Star Trek* say, "Resistance is futile."

I said, "Why don't you talk to Dick?" Dick Costolo was our friend before we first asked him to be an angel investor and later hired him. He and Evan were good buddies. They respected each other's work, and they often hung out together—sometimes they even met up in Vegas. Maybe Dick could help soften this blow.

I continued: "Tell Dick you will support him not as *interim* CEO but as the new CEO. Tell him you'll endorse him, and ask if he'll name you chief product officer. Then you can run Product, which is what you really like to do anyway. If you're not happy running Product, you can quit later, on your own terms."

If Evan simply moved positions within the company, it wouldn't be seen as a dramatic ouster. Then, if he later departed from the position of chief product officer, so what?

Ev was slightly comforted by this plan, but pulling it off was going to take some finessing.

Evan went into a conference room with Dick to discuss the plan we'd come up with. Outside the room, we could hear a lot of "no fucking ways" coming through the door. Ev came out looking very morose. With a cracking voice, he said, "I need to get some air," and left.

Now it was my turn to try. I went into the room with Dick, closed the door, and said, "What just happened?"

Dick said, "Evan wants to fucking horse-trade with me. I'm not getting the role of CEO through some kind of fucking deal."

I said, "Why not?"

He said, "I won't do it. I'm very uncomfortable with this plan. I won't do it."

I said, "That's disappointing. Ev's a good product guy. You want him on your team, don't you?"

He said, "Of course I do, but this is the board's decision."

I could see that Dick wasn't going to agree.

We all joined up again in the meeting room—Dick, Jason Goldman, Amac, Ev, and some of our communications people. The idea now was to come up with the communication strategy for Ev's departure. We had tried our plan, and it had failed.

But before we could get into it, I couldn't hold back. I thought of all the work that Evan and I had put into Twitter. I owed my success and my career to Evan, and I still felt I had much to learn from him. I thought about how few people there were in the world who could put up with me and find value in what I did the way Evan could. I honestly felt he was a good leader and that it's usually best if the CEO of a company is also its founder. He couldn't leave like this. It wasn't fair. Nobody was thinking about Evan as a person and what this would do to him and his career. It was killing me.

I said to Dick, "Wait a minute. I heard you, but for the sake of everyone here, I want to confirm this. You don't want to keep Evan on as chief product officer, with his full endorsement of you not as interim CEO but as actual CEO, and your reason for this is that you're uncomfortable. Is that correct?"

I had everyone's attention. As I thought he would, Dick confirmed what I had said: "Yes, it makes me uncomfortable."

Uncomfortable. It was such a weak emotion in contrast to what Evan was going through.

"How about this?" I said. "How about you be a little fucking uncomfortable for your friend. For your fucking friend. A little uncomfortable."

There was a long, silent moment. Then Dick said, "All right, I'll fucking do it."

There was more back-and-forth, Dick spoke to the board, and eventually everyone agreed. It was settled. So Dick ultimately came through for Evan. I kind of shamed him into it, which didn't feel good, but I felt I'd accomplished a small victory for my friend. Ev could walk away from Twitter on his own terms. He more than deserved that.

Beyond what it meant for Evan, the change in management was a sign for me. My perhaps overly happy-go-lucky optimism and change-the-world idealism was out of place in a company where the leadership was in flux and my friends were in conflict. I didn't like to force an issue, and the fact that I had to in that case meant we weren't all seeing eye to eye.

All kinds of crazy stuff had happened, and continued to happen. Jack had been yanked from CEO to be replaced by Evan. Two years later Evan was booted; he stayed as chief product officer for six months, three of which he was on leave, and then quietly left. A couple of weeks after the dust settled on Evan's departure, Jason Goldman got his own marching orders. Relationships were destroyed. Jack and Ev were no longer friends. Jason Goldman and Dick Costolo weren't too friendly, either. Even my friendship with Jack was strained for a bit, though never broken. It was a trying time. During those turbulent days, I remember sitting in a board meeting and thinking to myself, *Why is all this happening?* And then the answer dawned on me. *Oh. Because billions of dollars are now involved.*

It's a little abnormal to have three CEOs in three years, but the turbulence at Twitter was the reality of what happens when a startup is successful. The stakes are higher. The board of directors was made up mostly of investors. They had no ability to redesign the product or write code to fix a problem. The power they had was to reorganize the leadership.

The changes looked like power plays. They looked calculated from some perspectives, but I don't believe anybody was being malicious. If you were to talk to any of the people involved, they'd say they were doing what they thought was best for the company. Our success meant the stakes were higher now. People became opinionated. It provoked action, and there were casualties.

———

Ev was gone. Jack was gone. Jason was gone. All were off exploring new projects and opportunities. I started to get restless. Think of the effect of surface area on a melting ice cube. If you want the ice to melt faster, you break it up to expose a greater surface area to the warmer air than would be exposed if you left the ice in a solid block. The same is true if you're trying to effect more positive change. Theoretically you should start multiple successful companies and then leave them to smart people to run. Some would argue that it makes the most sense to pick one and do it really well, but for my purposes (spreading = good), I thought the surface area approach made the most sense. Maybe it was time for me to find my next project.

———

I had announced that I was leaving and had one foot out the door in 2011 when Amac, our general counsel, pulled me aside. Amac knew how hard I'd worked in the past five years to establish that Twitter was a neutral force in the world. The company might be involved in controversy, but we were not opinionated. We didn't take sides. It was *our* software, but *their* problem. The only, very narrow rules we had for kicking people off the service were directly derived from actual laws.

Now Amac said, "I know how sensitive you are about separating Twitter and the government..." Then he told me that Twitter was planning to host a presidential town hall meeting. People on Twitter would be able to ask Obama questions. There would be a separate website for it, and a moderator.

After a bit of thought, I said, "That's fine. It's similar to the one-off micro-websites we did for the Super Bowl, the 2008 election, and other events. The only thing is the moderator shouldn't be someone from Twitter. We can't have a Twitter employee standing next to the president. It should be a news-person, an anchor, or a pundit. If we don't participate, then we're just the tool. They could be using the telephone."

Amac agreed, and everything was set—or so I thought.

June 28, 2011, was my last official day at Twitter. The next day, Twitter's government and politics guy at the time sent out a company-wide email, "At 8 a.m. PDT tomorrow, the White House will be announcing its first-ever 'Twitter town hall' with President Obama. The event is scheduled for next Wednesday, July 6, at 11 a.m. PDT and will be streamed live from the East Room of the White House. Jack Dorsey will be the moderator." (One of Dick Costolo's first decisions as CEO had been to bring Jack back into the leadership fold of the company in a very public way, though soon Jack's focus seemed to shift back to Square.) I read this email first thing in the morning, in bed, on my phone. I was horrified. I imagined Jack standing next to the president as if to say, "Not only does Twitter love the U.S. government, but we love Obama!" This was exactly what I'd worked so hard to avoid.

Without pausing for reflection, I hit Reply All and wrote:

When Amac first explained this to me he said that nobody from Twitter would be the moderator specifically to highlight the fact that we are a neutral technology. I very strongly disagree with anyone from Twitter being involved as the moderator especially a founder.

This is very wrong and I've made my case many times. Please work harder to get a proper moderator from a well-respected news organization. Not our founder in charge of product. This goes against three years of work to stay out of the narrative and remain neutral.

Amac, what happened? This is the complete opposite of what you pitched me and it was the one thing I said to avoid with which you wholeheartedly agreed. The only thing I said to avoid. Please, please, please don't do it this way. We should not get involved in this manner.

Biz

To be fair to Amac, I am not sure who made the decision to change what he and I agreed upon—but I was angry. During the Arab Spring it had been so hard to keep us neutral—to diplomatically dodge all those land mines. All those years of work were going to be undone in one day. Replies to my impassioned email immediately came in, many in support of my statement, some asking me if I was aware that I'd sent my criticism to the entire company. Damn, yes.

I was still technically an adviser to Twitter, but it wasn't my call. They had Jack go ahead with the town hall. And that was my last all-company email.

Ultimately, a decision like the choice of the town hall moderator comes down to a question of PR versus philosophy. The Twitter I helped build had an idealistic long-term vision. We were in the business of uniting humanity. In fact, I hired a corporate social responsibility person several years before I hired a sales person. The highest value I saw in Twitter was its ability to transmit information immediately and to help people react quickly and together in critical times or sometimes just for fun. If there was an earthquake, a revolution, a triumph, a party—what could Twitter do? In my view, Twitter didn't take sides. We stayed out of controversy. This neutrality allowed the service to work across cultures and religions, and to be truly democratic.

My job had always been to say what the company did and why. I was the idealist. I wasn't politically motivated, and I wasn't trying to make anyone look bad or good. It was my duty to sound the alarm about the town hall decision and anything else that I thought might jeopardize our mission, even if it was unpleasant. I like to think that I built a brand that is synonymous with freedom of speech and the importance of the democratization of information.

But it was Dick's company to run. I believed that doing good in the world was the key to Twitter's success. I wanted to redefine capitalism. By signing up for Twitter you were becoming part of something good. Dick had to lead a company with that kind of soul into a profitable business. No small task.

From the beginning, I had built a moral compass and righteous soul into the company. I had instilled in the company the spirit of doing well by doing good. I had done all I could personally in that regard. One of the last projects I had a say in was moving Twitter to new offices in San Francisco's Mid-Market area. At the time, this was a rundown part of the city where our presence could make a difference. Indeed, after

Twitter moved, other companies soon followed suit, starting the revitalization of the neighborhood.

Now it was up to Dick to grow the business and to keep that spirit alive. It was up to me to hope that our early investment in altruism would grow along with the company.

Here I was fighting little skirmishes. That wasn't how I wanted to spend my time. I trusted that, overall, Dick and the company had the right instincts. Business was thriving, and the spiritual backbone was in place. Twitter was set up for success. It was time for me to do a whole other thing. They had this.

——

At Blogger, my colleagues and I developed a talking point that summed up our beliefs: "The open exchange of information can have a positive global impact." We had taken that with us to Twitter. In fact, that aphorism became a tacit, qualitative initiative. We could have said our mission at Twitter was "To increase the open exchange of information for positive global impact." After six years, hundreds of millions of active users, and billions of Tweets every day, we could have declared our mission accomplished.

When I left, Twitter was not just successful. It was also the empathetic company I wanted it to be. Instead of moving down to Mountain View like many big tech companies, they'd made the decision to move into a derelict neighborhood in the center of San Francisco. Dick and the leadership formed a special team to engage actively with the community and figure out how Twitter could best help improve it. In my final days at the company, they were completing that agreement. In the fall of 2010, only six months after releasing its first advertising product, the company launched Twitter Ads for Good. Through that program, nonprofit organizations apply to receive pro bono promoted Tweets and accounts.

Twitter was doing good, and it would keep doing good without me.

It was time for me to figure out what I wanted to do next. While I did so, I teamed up with Evan and Jason to noodle with no particular goal in mind. Reviving our old company name, the Obvious Corporation, we did some investing in startups. We talked about ideas for new companies. We hired an executive coach, who analyzed our strengths and weaknesses—how we could expand our abilities, double-down on things we were good at, and strengthen our weaknesses. Jason and I helped Evan start a publishing platform called Medium. Some entrepreneurs might take the time between startups to get an MBA or be an entrepreneur-in-residence. Instead, I did Obvious with those guys.

This interlude gave me time to distill some of the notions and theories I'd been working on over the years. We took a high-altitude, long-term view of what we, as entrepreneurs, were capable of doing in our city, in our country, and in our world. People are proponents of change; tools are helpful. We didn't know what we'd build, but we shared the desire to build systems that would help people work together to make the world a better place.

I ruminated on all the principles I'd been implementing at Twitter: empathy, altruism, humanity. Through DonorsChoose.org, Product(RED), and my involvement with other charities, I had realized that helping other people was fulfilling. It gave my life meaning. Above all, I had learned through Livia's daily example. In her work at WildCare, she'd been bucked in the stomach by a deer, sprayed directly in the eye by a skunk, taloned in the face by an owl, and she'd given mouth-to-mouth resuscitation to a squirrel. Through it all, and every day since, I'd watched her glow with empathy and selflessness. Being around her all the time, I can't help but soak that up. I might be a decent guy, but it's because I'm deeply influenced by her.

This realization led me to define my life's work. I knew what I wanted my work, my direction, and my legacy to be. I decided to dedicate my life to helping people. But it had to be via something I was good at.

Our approach to work, the projects we select, and the little things we do each day all add up to a whole greater than the sum of its parts. If philanthropy or charity or goodness—call it what you will—is woven into the fabric of a business, then you automatically do good as you make your way. I wanted to redefine the success metrics of capitalism according to the definition I'd been developing at Twitter. First, having meaningful, positive impact. Second, truly loving our work. Third, generating strong revenues. This is how corporations can best achieve compound impact in the world. We can do well simply by doing good. It is possible for us to work toward creating a healthier planet, a smarter world, even better humans.

I wanted my next project to manifest all that I believe.

18

THE TRUE PROMISE OF A CONNECTED SOCIETY

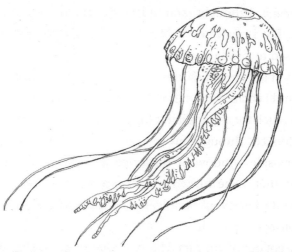

My son, Jake, was born in the early hours of November 21, 2011. Later that morning, when Livy was comfortable in the recovery room, she lifted me from my helpless, though elated state by making a request.

"Go out," she said, "and please get me a decaf soy latte and fruit."

It had been a sleepless night. I was overtired (if a husband is allowed to say that the day after his wife gives birth) yet buzzing with energy. Reciting the instructions in my head so I got the order right, I jumped into Livy's Subaru Outback. *Fruit, soy latte, fruit, soy latte, fruit...*

Near the Marin General Hospital is a plaza with a Starbucks. I turned into the parking lot behind a brand-new black Prius. Suddenly, the Prius stopped. There were five empty spaces up ahead, but the driver was waiting for someone with a grocery cart to unload one million bags into her car. *You gotta be kidding me.*

Screw it, I thought, and pulled around the left side of the Prius. But I neglected to factor in the size of Livy's Subaru. I'm used to driving my little car, a Mini. The hulking Subaru didn't fit between the Prius and the line of parked cars on my left, and I scraped the side of the Prius.

So much for a quick jaunt to Starbucks.

I looked through my passenger-side window into the driver's-side window of the Prius. An ancient woman was sitting there. She turned to me, looked right into my eyes, and said, "Fuck you, asshole." I couldn't hear her, but I had no trouble reading her lips.

We got out of our cars. The woman was very upset. She continued swearing at me, a lot.

Trying to calm her, I said, "Everything's going to be okay. This is just a scratch. The cars can easily be fixed. I will pay for it. Here's what I'm going to do. I'm going to write down my insurance information for you."

I wrote down my phone number, my full name, everything I thought she needed. While I was writing, I said, "By the way I'm actually coming from the hospital. My wife just had our first baby. It's a boy." I was trying to be extra nice. I'd caused her trouble, but I was going to fix it. I thought a little small talk would help her calm down. "I wish we were meeting under nicer circumstances," I said. "You seem like a nice person."

She said, "Did you say you had a son?"

An image of Livy sprang to mind, holding the little wrinkled bundle that was Jake. I was a *father*. I had a *son*.

I smiled. "Yeah."

She said, "Well, that's *my son's* car you fucked up," and returned to screaming at me.

When I got back to the hospital, the nurses asked what had taken so long. I told them I'd crashed the car. They loved that and mocked me for making a rookie father mistake.

It's a small moment. A frazzled new father. A cranky old woman. A fixable problem. All day long we make choices that have consequences, and above all the choice that interests me most is how we interact. Do we hear each other? Can we find empathy? What does knowing a little piece of personal information change? If I find out why the old lady is so unhappy— she tells me she recently lost her husband—I can understand why she can't stop screaming at me for scratching her son's car. *This stranger just became a father; this is a big moment for him. This ancient woman lost her husband of sixty years last year; any inconvenience is the last straw for her.* The more connected we are, the more empathy we feel.

The internet and mobile devices have connected the world like never before. The onset of social media motivated another steep acceleration in connectivity. For almost a decade now, we've been "friending," "following," "liking," and in other ways amassing a prodigious network of virtual connections, but without a long-term goal. What's it all for?

Connections foster empathy. In the summer of 2008 a woman named Amanda Rose, while sitting down with some friends at a pub in London, had the idea to gather together a bunch of friends using Twitter. She decided to charge for the event and to ask for donations of canned goods, both in support of a local homeless shelter, The Connection. She named it the Harvest Twestival, and—boom!—in a single night she raised a thousand pounds.

Impressed by what she'd experienced, Amanda expanded her efforts. She said, "Hey, everyone in two hundred cities around the world, let's all host events and raise some money." Boom! She raised $264,000 for Charity: Water. She then decided to make a whole thing of it. And when I say "whole thing," I mean it. Twestival is now a global social media fundraising initiative, helping communities around the world use social media to create fund-raising events. Talk about compound altruism!

Twestival and other efforts like it prove that the flocking I observed back in the beginning of Twitter, at South by Southwest, is more than a way for a bunch of nerds to decide which bar to hit. It offers glimpses of what happens when random groups of humanity become one and *do something*. Back at SXSW, I saw flashes of a utopian future. Little daydreams can come true.

Imagine that kind of behavior on a six-billion-person scale. What if we weren't citizens of a particular country or state? What if we were citizens of the world? It's mind-blowing.

The creator of *Star Trek*, Gene Roddenbery, envisioned a utopian future in which humanity had eliminated hunger, crime, poverty, and war. Where we humans unite to explore the universe. How are we going to get there, or to a reasonable version of it, minus the evil Borg ("Resistance is futile")?

Technology is the connective tissue of humanity. Designed right, it can bring out the good in people. It can connect us into one giant, emergent, superintelligent life form. That's what I saw happening with Twitter.

Flocking is a triumph of humanity. It can make things happen. Imagine if humanity could cooperate like an emergent life form—we could get things done in a single year that would otherwise take one hundred years to do. Imagine if all the world's astrophysicists put their egos aside and collaborated on a Mars mission? Or all the environmental scientists worked as one on global warming? Or the world's best oncologists took on cancer together, one type at a time? Only 114,000 people in the world have thirty million dollars or more in assets. What if they were in a Google group and decided to invest in one thing to change the course of history?

Then there's all of us, and together we are more powerful than any one thing. Can you imagine what we could get done?

———

These ideas were rattling around in my head when I went for a walk with Ben Finkel. Ben and I have known each other since 2007, when a mutual friend introduced me as a potential

THE TRUE PROMISE OF A CONNECTED SOCIETY

adviser to his startup, which Twitter subsequently acquired. Ben and I liked to get coffee, walk around, and talk about ideas. One nice, sunny day in December 2012 we were walking around Yerba Buena Gardens, a park in San Francisco, talking about various things, when a thought popped into my head. It was as if my brain had asked me a question. The question was: If I had to build a search engine today, given today's technology landscape, what would it look like?

But not exactly a search engine. I put it in slightly different terms to Ben: "What if someone forced us to build a system that could answer any query you put to it? What if that was our challenge?"

How does a search engine work? Documents on the internet are hyperlinked. When you ask the search engine a question, it finds you a document that an algorithm has determined is most relevant to that question.

But now there is nearly one active mobile phone for every person on earth. Practically everyone has a mobile phone.

I started to answer my own question. "If we had to invent the search engine, we'd do it on mobile. Phones are the hyperlinks of humanity." My thought was at once simple and obvious, and at the same time exciting to both of us. People were already connected. All those friends and favorites and followers made up a network. A network that rivaled any search engine's ability to comb through documents with speed and accuracy. There was room to reinvent the whole idea of getting help.

Ben said, "Oh my God, you're right." And he had his own enthusiastic ideas for how this might work.

Then I said, "We could build a system in which you ask a question. The system will send it out to people in your social networks—maybe two degrees out. If they don't know the answer, they can forward it. It's guaranteed that someone knows the answer. It's six degrees of separation on hyper-speed. We could build a system to answer any query. We just need people to route the questions."

This kind of problem solving was something we already saw people trying to do by jury-rigging technology. They set up Yahoo groups; they ask questions on Twitter, Instagram, and Facebook. But there was no technology that let people answer one another's questions quickly and elegantly, without other distractions, on a mobile phone—with pictures to boot. Ben and I got really excited. An app that resembled a search engine that could answer any question because it sent it out to people—with real knowledge, real experience. It was better than artificial intelligence—it was *actual* intelligence. It might be the future of search. People helping people. It sounded like a thing! A startup! That was our walk.

The next day, I called Ben. "I'm still thinking about this."

He said, "So am I."

The simplest way to explain Jelly is that it's a tool for people to help one another.

It's not about technology. It's about people. It's such a simple concept. Forwarding a question to a friend who might know the answer. People helping other people is the coolest thing in the world. This idea makes use of our already connected society. How could all those friends, followers, and contacts help one another? This was what we'd all been working for: a way for us all to be citizens of the world.

Ben and I couldn't shake the idea.

We decided to name it Jelly because jellyfish have no brains. Instead, they have what's called a "nerve net." In the face of a challenge, it takes only one loosely connected neuron out of millions to fire, and suddenly many individual jellies become one and serve as a brain for the group. When the challenge has passed, the jellies go back to floating along, doing their thing.

Jellies have been around for about seven hundred million years (which is pretty good for something without a brain). But the idea that groups of individuals can accomplish something together that they cannot do alone because they can coordinate instantly via loose connections is a glimpse into the future.

This is how we envision Jelly working. Only now, in this unprecedented age of mobile connectivity, can a world of individual people instantly react to the questions of others in a way that makes the whole smarter than the sum of its parts. The true promise of a connected society is people helping one another. That's why we decided to make Jelly.

I ran the idea for Jelly by some of the people I most respect, secretly hoping they'd say it wasn't worth my time, because I knew that if I started this, I'd have to give it everything I had. I began with Jack Dorsey.

"Stop talking," he said. "It's uniquely suited to you. It's all the things you hold dear. You have to do it."

I tried it out on three friends I consider brilliant: Jack, Kevin Thau, and Greg Pass. I'd always referred to Kevin as "Twitter's most beloved employee." He joined in 2008 to run mobile strategy and wound up leading all our mobile initiatives. Greg Pass was a founder of Summize, and Twitter's first chief technology officer. All three of my guys were telling me I had to do it. And Ben Finkel wanted to quit Twitter and start it with me. Then Livy and I went to dinner at Kevin Thau's house. For the third time, he said, "So Jelly. I'm in."

I said, "Is that what the kids are saying these days? 'I'm in' means you think it's a good idea?"

He said, "It means I want to work with you."

Suddenly I felt sick to my stomach; I might actually have to go ahead with this. Kevin had twenty years' experience in the mobile industry. He's an all-around business athlete—a technical guy, a business guy. If I had the support of both Kevin and Ben, I knew I'd be capable of turning the idea into a bona fide company.

I'd always seen myself as Best Supporting Actor to Ev's Best Actor. Working with him had been amazing; it changed my life. I'll always consider him a good friend. But on my own now, I felt a new surge of self-confidence.

Still, part of me was disappointed. I liked working three days a week at Obvious and spending the rest of the time with my newly increased family. Hence the churning stomach. But I couldn't let this idea go. Jelly would let people help each other. It would be a mobile application that looked like a search engine, but there'd be a big difference—it would be people answering queries, not computers.

Wouldn't it be great if everyone were always able to hold in their minds the notion that there are people who need help? Wouldn't it be great if everyone were always able to hold in their minds the notion that there are people standing by to offer help?

The best swing you can take at global citizenship is to cultivate empathy. It all starts with the ability to place yourself in someone else's shoes. *This old lady is cursing at me because I scratched her car. I'm not going to yell back at her. I'm going to listen to her. I have my own whole thing going on right now, but there are other people besides me. They have problems; I can help them.* If you exercise that muscle, if everyone does, then we're headed in the right direction for the future.

Jelly isn't going to save the world, but maybe it will nudge the world toward greater empathy. I decided to give it a go.

I began my working life as Biz Stone, Genius. I knew that I was a guy who could do something, but I wasn't sure exactly who I was, what I believed, or what I wanted to accomplish.

Now I've figured out what I'm doing, and I've stopped calling myself a genius. Instead, I'm a guy who believes in the triumph of humanity with a little help from technology. It might not be as pithy or as grand as genius, but it means a whole lot more to me.

And so I created Jelly to carve its own specific niche in the world of technologies that connect humanity. Whether my new company will be a success is unknown, but it is driven by the principles that most inspire me.

I've said to our team that if we can get hundreds of millions

217

of people to enter into their daily muscle memory the idea of helping another person, we may be able to have a positive impact on the global empathy quotient. Jelly's big, aspirational vision of the future is to build worldwide empathy.

On some kind of cumulative, subconscious level, humanity has found its way into the most hyperconnected time in our history. We can share digital photos with a retro look, we can play games with friends of friends, and we can follow the pulse of the planet in 140 characters or less.

However, there is something far more important in store for humanity now that we live this way.

Why are we building vast personal networks? For most of us, this question is not the primary driver of our continued desire to tap the Follow button. We're not thinking about the long-term application of these connections. We mostly just want to share pictures with friends, get instant access to information, and so on. We want to play Letterpress and remember whose birthday it is. Instant access to information and people is fantastic. We've been doing interesting and fun things since the advent of this newfound connectivity. Nevertheless, I'm asking *why?*

Why have we become the most hyperconnected humanity that's ever existed on earth? It's not about keeping tabs on friends and family. It's not about playing games. It's not even about advanced information retrieval or staying informed about world events. The true promise of a connected society is people helping one another.

Again, people are basically good. We are connecting ourselves so that we can help each other. So we can collaborate. What better reason could there be?

We've all done this. Driving along the highway, we've spotted a person pulled over to the side of the road. Three things go through our mind in a fraction of a second. Fundamentally, people are good, so the first thought we have is *I should stop and help.*

But then we have other thoughts.

What if it's a crazy person?

I might get stuck here for hours.

I'll be late to where I'm going.

The third thing we do is tell ourselves a little lie. *They probably have AAA.* Or, *They probably already have a friend on the way.* Maybe even, *They probably have AAA and a friend on the way, so if I stop, I'll just be a nuisance.* Then we toss the guilt on our pile for the day and zoom on past.

But what if we stopped? What if we pulled over and asked, "What seems to be the problem? Oh, it's a flat tire? Do you have a spare? I can change that for you." Let's say we changed the flat tire, dusted off our hands with satisfaction, accepted a heartfelt thank-you, and went on our merry way?

How good would we feel? We'd feel amazing! *What a great person I am. I stopped and helped someone in need.* We'd be full of righteous pride. In fact, we'd find any excuse to share our humanitarian effort with others. "Oh, you guys drove to work today? That reminds me of how I helped this person…"

Everyone has empathy inside them, but sometimes it lies dormant until one has an eye-opening experience. They go to Africa. A doctor saves their child's life. A dear friend needs help. These are specific, unique situations that wake us to a new way of seeing the world. But how can empathy be awakened across whole societies?

If helping others were easy, we'd all do it a lot more. Stopping to change a flat tire takes time, expertise, confidence that you are safe, and possibly a change of clothes. The true promise of a connected society is enabling our dormant potential for empathy. It's leveraging all this mobile, social connectivity so that helping others becomes as easy as a thumb swipe. Jelly may not be the answer, or the only answer, but at least it's got the right question guiding it forward.

Global empathy is the triumph of humanity.

CONCLUSION

The bonds I made at Twitter are for life. I've orchestrated a few deals connecting charities like DonorsChoose.org and Product(RED) to Jack's company, Square. I'm on the board of Evan's company, Medium. Jack and Evan are angel investors and personal advisers to me for my company, Jelly. I hang out with both of them socially, separately, and see them each every week.

Twitter went public just as I was finishing this book. The company got a ton of attention in the press. Everyone was talking about Twitter. Twitter was trending on Twitter. Anytime a company goes public, there's a lot to say about it, but for me Twitter remains a simple tool that creates great opportunities. It certainly did in my case. I helped make Twitter, and as with all we experience, it helped make me.

I propose that the lessons in this book are core to almost any experience. If you look beyond the everyday of commuting, drinking coffee, working, drinking some more coffee, forwarding various emails among your colleagues, going home to the bills you can or can't pay this week, if you look past the grind, you will find truths about how and why you get up in the morning, and what infuses color into the black-and-white of reality. Passion, risk, originality, empathy, failure, optimism, humor, wisdom from others—these are the forces that drive our decisions, how we define success, and whether, in the end, our lives add up to a fulfilling whole. There may not be a specific day when you sit down and say to yourself, *Self, how can you find the bright spot in this situation?* but my hope is that these concepts will filter their way through the challenging moments and poke their heads into the cubicles, offices, living rooms, boardrooms, and bedrooms where paths are carved, directions are changed, and inspiration is born.

I invite you to open your mind to new possibilities. Let's fake it till we make it. Let's create visions of an aspirational future.

You don't have to quit your job. But think about what might change your trajectory by half a degree. It could be that when you come home every night your first words are "I'm home! How can I help?" Try doing that. You may have a shitty job. You don't like it. You do it for the money, even if the money isn't great. Try to look at your work in a different way. Find something about your life that's great. Follow that thread. Volunteer. Even if you're in the worst possible situation, there's hope. Challenge yourself. Set your own bar. Redefine your success metrics. Create opportunities for yourself. Reassess your situation.

We are all marching together. We're headed toward something big, and it's going to be good.

ACKNOWLEDGMENTS

Getting work done at a startup can be difficult. There are many distractions. I've discovered over the years that one of the biggest distractions is me. I'm always talking, joking, sharing ideas, asking questions, and crossing personal boundaries in the name of innovation in a way that I think is "folksy," but it might not seem that way to everyone. In general, I tend to have an unsettling effect on the people around me. So, to everyone who has endured sitting next to me over the course of my career, I applaud and acknowledge your ability to focus.

To be more specific, aside from my beautiful, smart, loving wife Livia, I'd like to acknowledge a bunch of other people.

Thank you Mandy Stone, Margery Norton, Sarkis Love, Lucien Renjilian-Burgy, Joy Renjilian-Burgy, Donald Burgy, Steve Snider, Marc Ginsburg, Dan Godrick, Jason Yaitanes, Greg Yaitanes, Greg Pass, Jack Dorsey, Evan Williams, Sara Williams, Jason Goldman, Peter Jacobs, Hilary Liftin, Raymond Nasr, Ben Greenberg, Lydia Wills, Nicole Bond, Katie Alpert, Camille Hart, Lauren Hale, Steven Johnson, Stephen Colbert, Ron Howard, Charles Best, Chrysi Philalithes, Doc G, Arianna Huffington, Brian Sirgutz, Al Gore, Bill Clinton, Bijan Sabet, Bono, Reid Hoffman, Roya Mahboob, Kevin Thau, Ben Finkel,

ACKNOWLEDGMENTS

Brian Kadar, Alexa Grafera, Austin Sarner, Luke St. Clair, Ben Finkel, Steve Jenson, Jason Shellen, Noah Glass, Alexander Macgillivray, Yukari Matsuzawa, Abdur Chowdhury, Giorgetta and Leo McRee, Fritz Glasser, Meghan Chavez, Wellesley High School, and, just to be safe, my past, current, and future self.

To be clear, if you've actually read this book, then you know I rushed at the very last minute. And the actual last minute—or past that—to write the acknowledgments. That means I probably forgot names instrumental to my success. You don't get to the level of success and happiness I've achieved without the collaboration of hundreds—possibly thousands—of people.

So, if I forgot to mention you by name, I thank you. What goes around, comes around. If you helped me, please know that I appreciate it, I wish you goodwill, happiness, and health.

Thank you,
Biz